All the Best

Sen George Mc Manus J.

The Boy
from Archie

The Boy from Archie

SELECTED AND ASSORTED MEMORIES

SENATOR GEORGE A. MCMANUS JR.

ARCHIE PRESS
Traverse City, Michigan

Published by Archie Press
Traverse City, Michigan

Publisher's Cataloging-in-Publication Data
McManus, George A.

    The boy from Archie : selected and assorted memories / George A. McManus. – Traverse City, MI : Archie Press, 2008.

    p. ; cm.
    ISBN: 978-0-9800665-0-0

    1. McManus, George (George Alvin), 1930- . 2. Legislators—United States—Biography. 3. Traverse City (Mich.)—Social life and customs. I. Title.

JK1319.M36 2008
328.73073—dc22   2007908030

Project coordination by Jenkins Group, Inc
www.BookPublishing.com

Printed in the United States of America
12 11 10 09 08 • 5 4 3 2 1

Dedication

This book is dedicated to a number of people since no man does anything by himself.

To Betty Seats and Joan Send, who typed the manuscript, and to Anne Boyles and Rebecca Chown, who edited the book.

To my parents, grandparents, great-aunts, and great-uncles, as well as my brothers and sisters and aunts and uncles, who by oral tradition provided some of the tales within this book.

To my teachers, who provided me the formal education to carry me through life. I would especially like to mention Mrs. Lenora Pitcher of the country grade school, Father Joseph Kohler and the Dominican Sisters of St. Francis High School, and Dr. Alvin Kenworthy, my major professor at Michigan State University.

To my many friends, fellow farmers, business associates, classmates, and others who advised me along the way.

To the extension crew of Art Glidden, Clarence Mullet, Andy Olson, Edna Alsup, Ruth Hunsburger, Walter Kirkpatrick, Stan Ball, and others who guided me through my early years in extension.

To Governor John Engler, Lieutenant Governor Connie Binsfeld, and Senators Henry Gast, Joe Schwartz, Joel Gougeon, Joanne Emmons, Dick Posthumus, and others who helped me politically as well as all my local supporters.

To my constituents throughout northern Michigan, who had faith and trust enough in me to elect me to the Senate.

To my wife Clara, who partnered with me through all the successes and failures in my life.

Finally, this book is dedicated to my nine children, who endured all my time away from home, to my twenty-three grandchildren, and to my three great-grandchildren, as well as all those to come. There are stories in this book that will provide you historical prospective on where you come from, or as my German great-grandmother would say when one of my aunts or uncles showed up with a beau, "Vas ist in zie beheint?" (*What kind of people do you come from?*).

Contents

Introduction ix

Chapter One
Family Beginnings. 1

Chapter Two
Early Days on the Old Mission Peninsula 35

Chapter Three
Local Communication and a Little Local Culture 53

Chapter Four
Local Geography and Related Stories 69

Chapter Five
Agriculture and . . . Yep, Related Stories 83

Chapter Six
Language, Nationality, Religion,
and All That Came with It 107

Chapter Seven
My Childhood through the First Years of Marriage 123

Chapter Eight
Politics and Humor 155

Chapter Nine
Family Fun on a Trip to Ireland 173

Chapter Ten
A Few Personal Profiles and Various Final Stories. 183

Introduction

This book is a series of short stories that encompass my memories of growing up on the Old Mission Peninsula. Many are historical, as recounted by my parents and grandparents about life in the 1800s and early 1900s as pioneers in Grand Traverse County.

Geographically, the book centers on the Archie neighborhood of the Old Mission Peninsula. The Archie neighborhood is the section south of Island View Road in Peninsula Township, which today is represented only by Archie Park.

I was born at home and spent the first twenty-five years of my life there. These early narratives are followed by some of the experiences I had in education, public service, and politics, all of which kept life interesting. Although it isn't the kind of stuff that made headlines, my experiences helped form the personal guidelines I used to work with all kinds of people.

Being Irish, I can't help but have some humor in this book. Oral tradition is part of the Irish psyche and has been a trademark for generations, mostly out of necessity. However, with television, radio, computers, and email, many people don't have time for the kind of oral historical lessons I received from my family.

This book is an attempt to record at least a few of these stories for the sake of history, so they aren't lost forever.

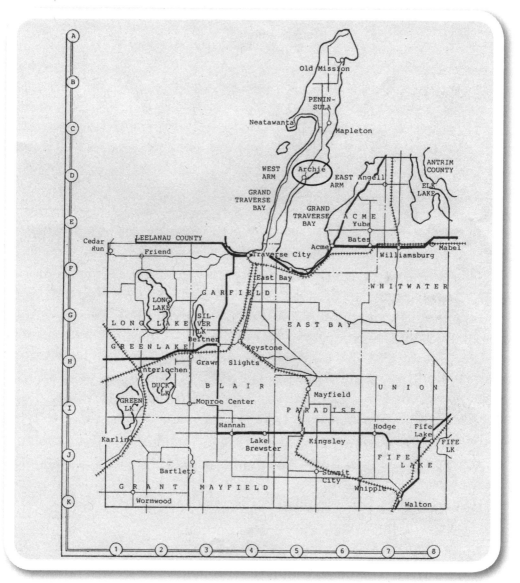

At one time there were four post offices on the Old Mission Peninsula. One was at Archie, the neighborhood where I grew up. The post office was named after a child of the first postmaster, Warren, who died prematurely.

Chapter One
Family Beginnings

The McManuses

It all began in 1867 when my great-grandparents, Thomas Arthur McManus and Mary (Beattie) McManus, sailed from Canada to Bowers Harbor on the Old Mission Peninsula. Thomas Arthur had been baptized in the Church of St. Anicet, Quebec, in August of 1835. His father was James McManus and his mother was Nancy Crowley.

My grandfather McManus, Thomas and Mary's son, always said his father came from Dundee. The only Dundee in Canada I've been able to find is a small village south of Montreal near the New York border in the province of Quebec. I learned there is a history of McManuses in that area.

Mary, Thomas Arthur's wife, had two sisters from Montreal who came to the Old Mission Peninsula at one time to visit her. They were all Montreal-area people including their father, Arthur Beattie. Both James McManus and Arthur Beattie are listed as farmers in *The Sellar's History*, a history book of that area.

Curiously enough, my great-grandfather originally traveled to California in one of the gold rushes but returned to Canada before setting off for Michigan. The story goes that he was a pleasant young fellow before he made the California trip. His father was quite a drinker, but Thomas Arthur had habitually smashed the bottles of whiskey when he was a boy and by all reports was an outstanding young man. Somehow the trip to California affected him and he was troubled later in

1

life. In spite of this, he and Mary raised a sizeable family of five boys and two girls.

Old Thomas Arthur was a big, broad-shouldered man, quite large in size, while Mary was a smaller, wiry woman. They were fortunate to be sailing to Bowers Harbor from Canada with a team of horses in their possession. A big storm blew up on the way over and the captain of the ship tried to get Thomas Arthur to cast his horses overboard, but he refused to do it. He said he'd throw over the harness to get rid of weight, but he wouldn't throw over the horses. He stood firm,

On the far right are my great-grandparents, Thomas Arthur and Mary (Beattie) McManus. To their left are James McManus and Hannah (Beattie) McManus, two brothers married to two sisters.

and so he had a team of horses when he got to Bowers Harbor. Once there, he purchased eighty acres located just behind the present Bowers Harbor Inn from a man by the name of Richard Johnson. My cousin Harold "Jolly" McManus Jr., a descendant, lived on that original property until he died.

One of the reasons Thomas Arthur settled where he did had to do with water. That particular property on Devils Dive Road where the old house was built sat near a spring. In those days, settlers tried to build near a source of water, because otherwise you either had to draw the water from the bay or dig a well with a shovel, which was a rather complicated and expensive process.

Thomas Arthur McManus had a brother, James McManus, who married Hannah Beattie, sister to Mary Beattie; James and Hannah farmed north of Bowers Harbor on the road to where the Peninsula Fruit Exchange is now. The brothers also had a sister in Michigan, also named Hannah, who married Wil Johnson and settled on Craig Road on the Old Mission Peninsula. There was also a brother, Hugh, who stayed in Canada and a sister, Rose, who married an O'Leary and moved to Ohio, plus older brothers Barnabas and John, Canadians.

The Idaho Story

Thomas Arthur and Mary McManus had seven children. The boys were Alfred, Henry, Wilford, George, and my grandfather, Arthur, and the girls were Addie (or Ada) and Janie. Great-grandmother Mary's youngest child was the first George McManus recorded in the United States in our family. When he reached eighteen years of age, when she was about sixty years old, she decided to take several members of the family—Alfred, Henry, Wilford, George, and Addie—to Idaho to homestead. This was about 1900, and I have copies of the original deeds that were eventually awarded in 1905 to her and some of the other members of the family from President Theodore Roosevelt.

I have never uncovered exactly how Mary and company went to Idaho, but I suspect it was by train. They headed to Boundary County, the northernmost county in Idaho, right next to the Canadian border, and homesteaded on the south edge of the county. The property is in the Pack River Valley, north and west of the town of Samuels, north of the town of Coeur D'Alene. I don't know how she found out about the property, or perhaps how the family did, but she homesteaded eighty acres, with son Alfred homesteading eighty acres as well.

Henry had married Annie Raftery from Manton by this time. As far as we know, they never had any children. After their time in Idaho, Henry and Annie eventually moved to Haver, Montana, near the Canadian border, and retired and died there. I only met Henry once. He came back to my grandfather's place sometime in the 1930s. Surprisingly, he was a bigger man than my granddad.

Wilford, I never met. He had a piece of property on the Old Mission Peninsula originally, part of the old homestead. He sold it to Coolidges, went West, and stayed there. As far as we know, he never had any children and ended up in northern California, but I've often wondered if the Patrick McManus who's the comic writer for the sports magazines might be some offspring of his. The sense of humor seems similar to the rest of us.

While in Idaho, Addie met Charlie Coolidge, who also had a homestead there. They got married by the Catholic priest in a town called Rathdrum, the county seat of Kootenai County. Eventually they came back to the Old Mission Peninsula with their homestead money.

George, the youngest great-uncle of mine, died on that homestead in Idaho of diphtheria. He got sick in the wintertime and they were unable to get him any medicine. When he died, they took some rough boards off the side of the cabin and built him a box and buried him there.

I once made a trip with my cousin John Gallagher and our wives to that particular area to try to find the properties our family homesteaded. We think we got pretty close, but I don't think we actually got on the properties because they're mostly wooded again now.

The idea back then in that heavily forested part of the country was for people to go in and homestead unclaimed land. To "prove up the claim," homesteaders had to build a cabin and live on the property for five years, clear five acres or so, and start farming. What many homesteaders ended up doing was building a cabin, clearing some land, proving up their claim, and upon receiving the deed from the government for the property, selling it to a timber company, who subsequently came in and logged it.

Great-grandma Mary was a typical homesteader. Her sons Alfred, Henry, Wilford, and I suppose George in the beginning would travel to the wheat fields in Montana and work for cash money while great-grandmother stayed in Idaho on the homestead, as was required in order to prove up the claim. She kept the home fires burning, you might say, until the boys returned.

One of our much-loved family stories goes that while the boys were gone to the wheat fields one year, a man came from out east and decided he was going to take over Great-grandma's claim. He set about building himself a cabin on the back side of the property, cleared some of the land, and began to prove up the claim. One night he was down at the bar in town and the bartender asked him, "Don't you know that property belongs to Mary McManus? That's her claim."

The stranger, the outsider, said, "No gray-haired old lady is going to chase me off the claim. I'm going to have that land."

Word got out, and Great-grandma let the boys know they'd better come home to take care of this problem. When they returned, they had a little meeting to decide what to do. Uncle Alfie always said, "And then all the rest of the boys had their rifles, and sure, I had my .22." He always had a little .22 he hunted with.

The boys started off across the woods. The stranger heard them coming and took off. My great-uncles smashed the cabin he'd built while the stranger headed to town to catch a train. He stopped in the bar for a much-needed drink and the bartender said to him, "What do you think of that little gray-haired old lady now?" Needless to say, the man left town and they didn't have any more trouble with anyone trying to take their claim away from them.

The life they led in Idaho was pretty wild. Another story fondly told is of the night Wilford and Henry were coming back from the wheat fields, walking down the railroad tracks toward the homestead. Highway robbers used to be pretty common in those days, so as they walked down the track, Henry said to Wilford, "Before we get to the woods, we'd better put the money where no one can find it."

They took off their shoes and socks and put the money at the soles of their feet, pulled their socks back on, and put on their shoes. Sure enough, as they were going down the track, a robber came out of the woods and stopped them. The boys told him they didn't have any money, but the man knew they were coming home from the wheat fields and that meant cash. He examined them all over and found nothing, but he knew they had to have money somewhere and he wouldn't let them go. He held a gun on them until finally Wilford said he had to go to the toilet.

That's where the highwayman made his mistake. He told Wilford to go up over the hill to relieve himself. The minute Wilford got over the hill, he headed straight for town. Henry got away too and was soon right behind him. The two of them ran all the way to Samuels, straight to the stationmaster's. In those days the stationmaster took care of the train but was also the law, and the boys told him what had happened.

It wasn't too long before the highwayman himself came walking out of the woods and down the track. The stationmaster went out to stop him and the highwayman reached for his gun. The stationmaster shot him on the spot and that was the end of that!

Family stories also involve mountain lions in the area. At night, when the boys would walk from Samuels back to their cabin, sometimes they would see mountain lions on the trail, in the light of the lantern. Wilford, always the hothead of the bunch, was walking along one night with Alfred when they came upon on a mountain lion lying in the middle of the trail. Wilford drew his gun to shoot it but Alfred told him not to. "You might wound it, and there's nothing worse than being in the woods in the middle of the night with a wounded mountain lion." So they waited most of the night until the mountain lion decided to get up and leave, and then they went on up the trail to the cabin.

Addie, the boys' sister, worked in a restaurant in Samuels. After she married Charles Coolidge, they worked hard to prove up their claim. Great-grandma and Alfred got their deeds from the federal government in 1905 and Great-grandma promptly turned around and sold her eighty acres to a timber company for the sum of two thousand dollars; I've got a copy of the deed.

Uncle Alfie sold his homestead as well, but his eighty acres contained quite a bit of cedar so he got more money than Great-grandma; he got $3,500. They each took their homesteading money and came back to the Old Mission Peninsula, where Uncle Alfie used his money to buy the forty-five acres I was raised on. He bought that property from George Carroll and also built the barn we housed our cattle in when I was a kid.

Great-grandma used her money to build the house on that property. The Swedish men in the neighborhood were good carpenters and had built several houses locally, so she hired one of them, Mr. Benson. She lived in that house with Alfred until she died in 1917 at the age of seventy-nine. I was raised in that house, the first house on the east side of the highway on the north side of Carroll Hill.

In addition to her Idaho experience, there are other interesting stories about Great-grandma Mary. She didn't go out to Idaho until she was sixty, so she was about sixty-five when she came back and built her house. One story goes that she was out picking cherries (this was

This is where I grew up on the north side of Carroll Hill on the Old Mission Peninsula. The home was built in 1906 by my great-grandmother Mary McManus with money from the sale of homestead property in northern Idaho.

after she was seventy years old!) one mid-day, standing on a ladder, when the ladder slipped out from underneath and caught her arm in the crotch of one of the limbs of the trees. She hung there until noon, when her son Alfred came in from the field for dinner. He found her dangling and got her down and she survived all right.

My granddad, Arthur, had a great love for his mother and she for him. They used to visit quite a bit. He lived a mile south on Carroll Road but passed her house on the way to church on Sunday.

The final story our family tells about Great-grandmother Mary is a bit superstitious,maybe, but you've got to realize these people were Irish, so the connections between the natural and the supernatural weren't that far apart. Great-grandma died in the bedroom on our old home farm. The family were gathered around the bedside when all of a sudden a bird appeared over the head of the bed. Uncle Alfie exclaimed, "The bird! Grab the bird!" There weren't any windows open in the bedroom, but when someone reached for the bird, it was gone. Everyone looked down and Great-grandma was dead. The family knew her soul was being carried to heaven by the bird.

Though great-grandmother was dead, the interesting circumstances surrounding her continued. Quite a saintly woman, she requested that she be buried with no flowers but rather a shock of wheat on her casket. She also didn't want to be buried in the Catholic cemetery at Mapleton, because she felt her marriage was a failure, so she was buried in Traverse City. Oddly enough, when I tried to find the gravestones of my great-grandparents, which should have been in the Catholic cemetery at Mapleton where some of the original settlers were, I discovered that neither of the McManus great-grandparents were buried there. The Carrolls are, the other side of my family, but not the McManuses.

The story goes that Thomas Arthur McManus was buried in Traverse City after he died in 1915, but when my cousin Jolly was the Peninsula Township supervisor, he had a college student do some investigating into the township cemetery at Ogdensburg on Center Road. He found that Thomas Arthur McManus was buried there in an unmarked grave. This made me do some investigating on my great-grandmother. The Traverse City Oakwood Cemetery records, not the regular cemetery book but an older one that goes clear back, indicates a Mary McManus was buried there for a time, but was eventually dug up and moved to Ogdensburg!

This corroborates to a certain extent another story the family has told for years, that Mary was originally buried in the St. Joseph Cemetery in Mapleton but her daughters had her dug up and moved to Traverse City to be alongside her husband, Thomas Arthur.

I suspect that's only partly right, because my information indicates they're both buried at Ogdensburg, which makes a lot more sense. Since they're in unmarked graves, we've never been able to find out for sure, but by piecing together both stories, a probable story emerges: we know Thomas Arthur couldn't be buried in the Catholic cemetery at Mapleton, by order of the priest at the time, so the family said they "took him to town." At that time, the Ogdensburg Cemetery was a Methodist cemetery and I don't expect the Catholic family wanted to admit he'd been buried there. "Taking him to town" (though no one said which town!) solved the problem.

When Mary was dug up and buried alongside her husband, the indication was she'd been reburied in Traverse City. But since she's not in the Oakwood Cemetery in Traverse City but at Ogdensburg, I'm sure the move was to bury the two of them together. Her daughters Addie Coolidge and Janie Buchan decided she should be buried with her husband. This was done not too long after she died in 1917.

Great-uncle Alfred inherited the house his mother had built with her homesteading money after she died. A lifelong bachelor, Alfie had been deaf from the age of seven. The story goes that his parents—my great-grandparents—sent him out barefooted to chase the cows early one morning when the ground was cold, and he developed some kind of cold that left him deaf. The only thing he could hear was the vibration in the air coming across East Bay from the noon whistle at the factory at Elk Rapids. We always had to talk to Uncle Alfie in sign language. I learned the alphabet in sign language when I was a young boy from my dad and granddad, and you should have seen Grandpa and Dad and Uncle Alfie sitting around talking to each other with their hands. Alfie could answer verbally, by the way. He could speak; he just couldn't hear.

In tracing the family genealogy further back from the Dundee part of Quebec, all indicators point to Ireland as the homeland. Of course,

"McManus" is an old, old Irish name dating back to the year 800 or so. "Beattie," my great-grandmother Mary's maiden name, is another old Irish name common in the Belfast area. Some of the family history indicates that one of my great-grandparents was a Highlander and another a Lowlander. Well, of course, the lowlands would be Scotland, and I'm pretty sure my ancestors didn't come from Scotland, although there are McManuses in Scotland. The McManuses in the Glasgow area of Scotland are McManuses who came from Ireland to Scotland anyway. The connection is more likely that Great-grandmother Mary was from the Belfast area and Great-grandfather Thomas Arthur from out in County Fermanaugh, County Roscommon, or County Down in Ireland where most of the McManuses originated. DNA, by the way, indicates County Down.

The Carrolls

Great-grandfather Edward Carroll on the other side of the family homesteaded 160 acres on the Old Mission Peninsula. He got a patent from Corporal Benoni Fosdick, who got the government patent from the War of 1812. Like my great-grandfather Edward, Fosdick was from Vermont. Somehow he'd gotten Fosdick to give—or perhaps he bought or traded—something for the patent on that 160 acres in section four of Peninsula Township. He married Jane Eliza Holman at Guelph, Ontario, and came to the Traverse City area in the late 1860s by way of Elora, Ontario. His father, Peter Carroll, came later and ended up a mile north on M-37 on top of Carroll Hill.

Peter followed his son to Traverse City and was actually married twice. His first wife, Dorothy Stevens, was from Vermont. He had twelve children by her, a sizeable family, and she died in Canada of "consumption," which I understand to be tuberculosis. Then, at an advanced age, still in Canada, he married a young lady from Ireland whom my dad always called Molly, but I think her name was Mary. He had three children by her, the youngest of whom was Charlie Carroll, the father to Bernie Carroll, who lived on the original Peter Carroll property at the top of Carroll Hill, across the road from the Chateau Grand Traverse winery on the peninsula.

They always tell the story that Molly Carroll cried for days and days after she came to Traverse City because they had told her that money grew on trees on the peninsula. She was bitterly disappointed to find out they were referring to apples and cherries rather than the actual coin!

This is a United States patent given to Edward Carroll, my great-grandfather, entitling him to 160 acres in section four of Old Mission Peninsula in 1868. It was issued as a result of the war of 1812.

Molly smoked a clay pipe, which was considered a bit unusual, but she was one hundred percent Irish, direct from the old country, and not a whole lot more than that was ever spoken about her or Peter Carroll. In *Sprague's History of Grand Traverse and Leelanau Counties*, published in 1903, both Edward and Peter Carroll's genealogies are fairly well documented, and I take what's written to be accurate. Peter is buried in the old Catholic cemetery in Traverse City as he died before there was a Catholic cemetery at Mapleton.

My cousin Jack Holman and I and our wives made a trip one time to Elora, Canada, to visit our Holman relatives. There are a sizable number of Holmans, my great-grandmother's maiden name, in the area still. We visited the library to check records and discovered several interesting facts: the land plats of the 1840s and 1850s indicated there were Holman, Buchan, and Carroll farms around the town of Elora just like there are today on the Old Mission Peninsula. In fact, the distances between them there aren't much different than they are here. These three families migrated into the Elora area and then migrated to the peninsula. Just why these people migrated from Vermont to Elora, I don't know, as well as why they migrated from Elora to the Old Mission Peninsula. The only information I have is the land patent, and it's rather interesting to speculate on how and why those moves were made.

Elora is located on a river with a waterfall, which provided power for a mill to grind grain, a pretty good explanation of why that town existed and why people might have migrated to it, but just why the other migration took place, I don't know. One thing is for sure: the border between Canada and the United States was not as tightly controlled in the middle 1800s as it is today and such movement was apparently fairly easy.

Edward Carroll had ten brothers. The story always went that "There were eleven brothers and they all had a sister, which made twelve in the family." The sister was Aunt Lizzie Buchan, the mother of Will and Frank Buchan. Will Buchan married Aunt Janie McManus and they had one child, Millicent, who married Amos Montague. Therefore, the descendants of Amos Montague are also relatives of ours.

Frank Buchan's son Lester married Florence Holman, which made the Buchan kids all double cousins of ours. The one in class with me was Bernice Buchan, who eventually married Marty Ghastin of Traverse City. Patty Buchan, another of their daughters, wrote the poem I've included below.

The Island in the Bay

The Indians tell the story of the island in the bay,
Of the squaw spirit who haunts it, sometimes by night, at times
    by day.
She carries her head beneath her arm, wandering to and fro,
Looking for her chieftain, who had her killed so long ago.
He wished to wed another, one so young and oh so fair,
Then the Indians left the island but the squaw's spirit lingers
    there.
The settlers came to take their place and fish from off its shore,
In the blue-hued waters of the bay, they fish forevermore.
Dick Basset was a fisherman of Civil War renown,
Thrice wounded, still he battled on to win that terrible war.
So great was his valour, he was granted the island's northern
    shore.
Frank Buchan came to help him from a mile across the way,
Summertime found them fishing 'round the island in the bay.
Then Dick went West and Frank was blest with a beautiful blush-
    ing bride,
They settled down to farm the land on the peninsula side.
They raised some crops and a family too, always with a beautiful
    view,
of the island in the bay.
Then Captain Webb came along with wisdom and foresight
He built a pavilion on the island for dancing late at night.
He took the dancers over in his ship *Chawauagon*
And when the dance was over, he ferried them home again.
The island has a history of which I here relate
But through it all, it has remained a wild and natural state.
If the swimming, fishing, and boating do not appeal to you,
You can always gain some pleasure from the most spectacular
    view.

On a calm and quiet day when the bay is serene
A reflection of the island in the waters can be seen.
There is a story too of treasure buried beneath its grounds,
But my feeling is the treasure is the pleasure that abounds
'Round the island in the bay.

Some have claimed it, some have named it,
But to me it will always be just "the island in the bay."

—Patty Buchan Tommey, cousin

As I said, Great-grandfather Edward Carroll had the 160 acres of hilly, sandy ground to start with. Great-grandmother Jane Eliza followed him a couple of years later when the log house was built. I have an interesting story about her coming to the peninsula. She came by train to Traverse City and started to walk the eight miles out to the homestead, carrying Great-uncle Lawrence, who had been born in Canada, on her back. As she got to the first bend on the peninsula, which would be three-quarters of a mile north of where the Congregational Church is now, she sat down under a tree to take a rest and a bear came out of the woods across the road. The Old Mission Peninsula in the 1860s wasn't quite as civilized as it is today! When Jane Eliza saw the bear, she walked to the top of the first hill and came upon a farmer milking a cow. He asked where she was going and she told him who she was and that she was headed out to the homestead on Carroll Road.

The farmer said if she'd wait a little bit until he finished milking the cow, he'd give her a ride. Sure enough, when he finished milking, he hooked the cow up to a wooden cart and toted her out to the Carroll homestead, and that's how Jane Eliza arrived on the peninsula.

I don't know whether Great-grandfather's native Vermont had convinced him you could farm hills or not, but he certainly did it. He really didn't know what he was getting into when he got the patent for that 160 acres, but there was a nice view of East Bay as well as a lot of timber on the land. In fact, it was virtually all timber, and probably most of it was white pine because the land was so light.

My great-grandparents, Edward Carroll and Jane Eliza (Holman) Carroll

I farmed on that land a lot when I was a boy. I don't want to say it was pure sand, but it was very, very close to it. On the east end, where my dad ended up, about twenty-seven acres out of forty-two were tillable.

Great-grandfather cut the timber off and eventually moved north to where Will Carroll's farm was at the east end of Island View Road on the opposite side of M-37. A good farmer, he accumulated quite a lot of land and was able to give some to each of his seven sons. Lawrence Carroll got a farm across from the Catholic Cemetery after selling his original land to the Coolidges, Steve Carroll got the farm on Island View Road, Andrew Carroll got the farm on the corner of Island View and M-37, Will Carroll got the forty acres on the east side of M-37 at the end of Island View Road, and George Carroll got the farm south of that, the one my folks bought from Alfie McManus. Alec Carroll, another son, got the south half of the original 160 acres, but he didn't stay there long. He married Daisy Johnson, who inherited some land from her father across the road from the Catholic Church where Tim Carroll is fixing up their old homestead now. Fred Carroll, Tim's father, farmed that land, and he got it from his father, Alec Carroll, but that farm really came through Alec's wife, Daisy Johnson Carroll.

John Carroll, another son, was to get the north half of the original homestead until he double-crossed his father in a timber deal.

The Johnsons were the original homesteaders of 160 acres just west of St. Joseph's Catholic Church and Blue Water Road. They sold the west eighty acres to my great-grandparents, Thomas Arthur and Mary McManus, in 1867, and kept the east eighty acres; Alec and Daisy raised their family on that piece rather than on the south eighty acres of the original 160 acres that Great-grandfather Carroll homesteaded on Carroll Road.

That leaves the daughters. Great-aunt Kate married a Bucere and they lived on Blue Water Road. Aunt Lizzie (Elizabeth) was married first to Matt Zoulek and then eventually to John J. Lardie. I don't know whether Great-grandfather provided them with anything or not. I doubt it. But neither did he in the case of my grandmother, Eliza Jane (Carroll) McManus, the third daughter. The farm that my grandparents ended up with was originally to go to John Carroll, my grandmother's brother, but they had to buy it .

John and his father, my great-grandfather Edward Carroll, logged off a chunk of that eighty acres one winter and John had the job of taking the logs to Traverse City. In those days a lot of that hauling was done after the bay froze over. If it was frozen with a good solid coat of ice, you could get a load of logs on the bay and have flat going all the way to Traverse City. If you had to take the road, you had hilly going. They did it both ways, but the bay was the easiest.

John delivered logs all winter to the mill in Traverse City. He had been given that farm, but with the idea that Great-grandfather would get the money from the logs. Well, in the spring of the year, when Great-grandfather went to collect the money, he found that John had collected the money on each load as it went in and spent it. There wasn't any money left, so John had to give the eighty acres back to him.

This explains how Grandpa and Grandma McManus ended up on eighty acres of sand hills in section four of Peninsula Township, the north half of the 160 acres that my great-grandfather Edward Carroll had homesteaded in the 1860s. It was not the usual thing for a farmer to provide his daughter with a farm in those days, though it was done for the sons. Nonetheless, my grandmother Eliza Jane did end up with eighty acres of her dad's farm, but not for free! When Great-uncle

John Carroll had to give the eighty acres back to his dad, Great-grand-father turned around and sold it to my grandparents for five hundred dollars when they were starting out in 1897.

My grandfather Arthur Thomas McManus, or A. T. as he was called, and his wife Eliza Jane (Carroll) raised eleven children on that eighty acres, seven boys (Verl, Harold, George [my dad], Bill, Elmer, Carl, and Huey) and four daughters (Marjorie, Margaret, Dorothy, and Norma). Their oldest two were Verl and Harold, Aunt Marjorie Gallagher

Taken in 1959, this photo shows four generations of McManus men. My grandfather T. Arthur is holding George III; on the right is my father George Sr., and I am standing on the left.

was number three, and my dad was number four, with seven more following.

They were able to give six out of the seven boys a piece of land. Verl and Harold each got twenty acres of the original eighty-acre McManus homestead on Devils Dive Road that my grandfather inherited from his mother. My dad got thirteen-plus acres in the back of the home farm, on Carroll Road. Uncle Elmer got thirteen-plus, and Uncle Bill got thirteen-plus of the east forty acres (the back end of the farm), part of which was eventually sold to Bob Bell. Brother Carl received the west forty acres with the buildings after taking care of my grandparents until they died, and he eventually sold to Bell as well.

Bell went on to start the subdivision on what we call the Bluffs, a piece of sand hill that was part of the old farm my granddad had, and also a part of the south eighty acres that great-grandfather'd had. It was kind of a high sand hill that rose up on all four sides. They've put up some very beautiful homes that look south on Grand Traverse Bay, and there aren't many places on the peninsula where you can do that. You usually look east or west or north, but not south.

Uncle Huey, the youngest boy, got a high school education instead of land. Aunt Marjorie married Cecil Gallagher and moved west of town; Aunt Dorothy never married. Aunt Margaret married Ben Hager, originally out of Fife Lake, and Aunt Norma married Bill Rasmussen, originally out of Cedar. The youngest daughter, Norma, ended up with a nursing education and became an RN.

Grandpa and Grandma McManus raised all those kids on that eighty acres they got because John Carroll decided to spend the logging money rather than save it for his dad, and you might wonder how they did it, but they all lived to a pretty ripe old age. Grandpa lived to be ninety-three and Grandma died at eighty-seven, old-time residents of the peninsula, on that original eighty acres they purchased from great-grandfather Edward Carroll.

It's interesting that my grandfather was always called "Arthur Thomas" and that in fact is the name on his tombstone, but if you go back to the records and investigate the name on his birth certificate, it's Thomas Arthur, the same as his father, and that is true for his marriage license as well. I expect what happened is they didn't want to call him "Junior," so somewhere along the line they turned the names around and began calling him "Arthur Thomas," or "A. T." I will refer to him accordingly, even though "Thomas Arthur" is technically correct.

Gramps only attended school up to the third grade. He went to the Mapleton School, about one-half mile east of where the McManus homestead was located, on what we call Devils Dive Road. He always told the story that since he only had one pair of shoes, he had to walk to school barefooted or in his stocking feet and then put the shoes on after he got inside the schoolhouse. The rule was you had to wear shoes during classes, and he didn't dare wear the shoes to or from school for fear he'd wear them out.

Both my granddads chewed tobacco; Grandpa McManus always chewed Peerless. That was his brand and it's the one thing he just had to have. In fact, when he was in the care facility just before he died, at ninety-three years of age, my cousin John Gallagher and I went up to see him. He was lying in bed and we asked if there was anything he needed. He said, "Reach over there, boys, in my draw [he always called a drawer a 'draw'] and fetch me a little Peerless. I think I'll have a chew."

A. T. and Eliza Jane were very poor people financially speaking, as were many others in the early days on the peninsula. Even though they were from old established families, there was not a lot of money and times could be very difficult. Their eighty-acre farm was on Carroll Road, just east of the Maple Grove School, though the original house was further south from where the houses are located today. It was about mid-point of the Carroll 160-acre homestead, next to Carroll Road, maybe a little bit toward the southern end on a hill that overlooked the whole 160 acres and East Bay.

Carroll Road, in the early days, went clear through. It left Center Road at the Maple Grove School and made the sharp bend at the end of the first forty acres and then went south past the acres originally owned by Great-grandfather Edward Carroll and then continued on to what we called the Bopry place at the bottom of Kelly Hill. Part of that has since been closed off, but in those days the road went clear through so it didn't make much difference where you built.

After the original home burned down, my grandparents built their second home further to the north, closer to Center Road, which meant better access to travel, but when they first married, they lived in the old log house that had been the original Carroll homestead.

The Fromholzes

My mother Frieda Anna (Fromholz) McManus was of German descent, so our family was always half German and half Irish, an interesting combination! In fact, my parents named their children accordingly. I'm George Alvin McManus Jr., named after my dad. My next brother is Francis (Frank) William McManus and he's named after my grandparents, William Fromholz and his wife Frances (Limburger) Fromholz. My sister Antoinette Louise was named after two of my mother's sisters, Louise and Clara Antoinette. My brother Michael (Mike) Anthony is named after my mother's grandfather, Antoinne Michael Limburger. My next brother, Dale Patrick (Patrick), is named for the Irish. My youngest sister, Frieda Ann, is named after my mother—and by the way, my mother was named after her grandparents, Ferdinand and Anna (Johanna) Fromholz. My brother Arthur Thomas is named after my grandfather, Arthur Thomas McManus.

My dad used to tell a story about something that happened on his wedding day that adds some evidence to the way families operated in those days. The great-grandparents, Ferdinand and Johanna Fromholz, gave my folks a dollar for a wedding present with a note to my mother that said, "Frieda, remember, you're always a Fromholz."

Great-grandfather Ferdinand Fromholz was a soldier in the Prussian Army and he married Johanna in Germany. In fact, they had two children there before they decided to migrate to the United States in the late 1870s. My great-grandfather, when he wasn't in the army, was an estate overseer between Berlin and Warsaw, Poland, in the area around Gruenwald. When they came to the United States, they came through the ports of Stettien and Hamburg in northern Germany. Ferdinand was from the village of Schoenbrun in Prussia while Johanna Dorothea Hanschke was from the village of Reigersdorf just east of Berlin. At the time of their marriage and eventual migration to the United States, they were living in the Berlin area.

Great-grandfather was six feet tall, but you had to be 6'1" to ride in the German cavalry. His brothers were that tall or better, so while they got to ride in the cavalry, he had to be an infantryman. He was never too happy about that. Later, when some of his family migrated to Brazil, he came to the United States.

He came first to Pittsburg, Pennsylvania, and had to decide where to settle. Most of the Germans were going to Wisconsin, but there was also land available in Blair Township in Grand Traverse County on Garfield Road. This was land the railroads had obtained from the government when they were putting in the rails. They were given every other section, and they were able to turn around and sell that land for farming and take the money and build tracks.

When it was time to make the decision, Michigan or Wisconsin, Great-grandmother Johanna said, "We go to Michigan, because it's closer to Germany." She always figured that maybe someday she'd get back to Germany. She never did, but that's how that branch of the Fromholzes settled in northern Michigan.

When they first came, they built a small house—"shack" would probably be a better word—near a spring on the north side of Garfield Road in section one of Blair Township where they could get water. They tell the story that it was cold enough the first winter that they had to sleep with the potato peelings they'd saved to plant in the spring to keep them from freezing.

Great-grandpa walked from that area to Elk Rapids each week, about twenty miles, to work in the pig iron factory. People who have been in the area a while remember the pig iron factory that used wood for fuel to make pig iron. Having soldiered in the German infantry, walking came naturally to him.

A hard-working pair of Germans who cleared the land and went about raising a sizable family, Ferdinand was tall and dignified and Johanna was rather short. They had eleven children, eight of whom who survived, including my grandfather, who looked after them for many years. They helped him buy the Flanigan farm next door to the land they eventually acquired and set him up in farming on that. He had to pay for the land, but they helped him get started.

They brought many customs with them from Germany that were quite different from the customs the Irish side of the family practiced. They made liverwurst, headcheese, sauerkraut, and all the various things Germans are known for. Johanna was an excellent cook, and that skill was passed on down through the family.

Lutherans from the northern part of Germany (Evangelish), Ferdinand and Johanna were founders of the Trinity Lutheran Church in

Traverse City and remained members all their lives. Their home was a place where many people came to visit, including ministers, judges, and individuals who had to make decisions about the future of the community. Great-grandpa was quite a respected advisor to many of these people, having been well trained in the military in Germany.

The Limburgers

Just across the valley on the next farm north, the Antoinne and Mary Limburger family settled. This set of great-grandparents originally came separately from Germany. Mary Limburger's maiden name was Englander and she came from the Strasburg area, sometimes in Germany, sometimes in France. Two of her uncles came from Germany to Utica, Michigan, and Mary came as a young girl as an indentured servant and had to keep house for them a number of years to pay for her passage.

Antoinne Limburger came from Baden in the south part of Germany, one of a sizeable family. He had been sent to a monastery to become a priest, and disliking that, had fled to England, where he got on a cattle boat and came across. The boat caught fire off the coast of Nova Scotia and burned, but he was rescued and came on to the United States.

Antoinne and Mary met in the Warren/Utica part of southeastern Michigan and were married there. Eventually they came to Traverse City because they were good friends of the Greilicks who had the mill at what's now known as Greilickville. They began working for the Greilicks, Mary as a cook in the boarding house for the men who worked in the mill while Antoinne had the job of keeping order and also going out into the farming area to buy produce for Mary to cook with.

Their oldest daughter we called Auntie (Anna). She married Dominic Rakowski eventually. My grandmother, Frances, was their youngest child. Several children in between died of the German measles and are buried in the Oakwood cemetery. Antoinne and Mary had a lot of misfortune, but the oldest and youngest daughters lived.

When my grandmother was a little girl, she used to play with the other children on the log pond at the mill in Greilickville. My great-grandmother felt this wasn't an appropriate place to raise a young child, so she decided they were going into the farming business. Accordingly, they bought a farm on Potter Road in section one of Blair Township and moved there.

My grandparents' home farms essentially joined each other and they eventually got acquainted and married and set up farming next door, where they carried on many of their family's German customs in cooking and farming and doing business. Grandpa was a moderator in the Haney School Board for many years and all their children were educated through grade school and some through high school. My mother, Frieda Anna, was the oldest child and she had one year of high school. Her sister Louise, who eventually married Bob Hall, had about the same amount of schooling. The younger ones, Clara and Harold and William Jr., or Billy, had high school. Harold married Dora Alpers and the youngest son, Bill, married Dolores Howe. I have several cousins on that side.

There was music and art on my mother's side of the family. My grandfather played the harmonica and my mother and her sister Louise both played piano. Actually, my mother took piano lessons from Sister Cecilia at the convent at Traverse City. My Aunt Clara (Moon) also turned out to be an artist, so there was a lot of education along those lines on that side of the family.

My German grandfather, Bill Fromholz, was pretty good at "turning the air blue" as they said in those days. If he got upset about something, he could swear like a trooper, in either English or German. He usually got over his anger fairly quickly, but he had the ability to let everybody around him understand when he was upset.

Grandpa Fromholz never raised much fruit in Blair Township. He had a few apple trees and a couple of cherry trees and periodically raised strawberries on a "pick your own" basis, but mostly he had cattle and hogs, raised corn and hay and potatoes, and sold cream. He raised cows just the same as they did on the peninsula and other places. They milked the cows, then separated the cream and took it to town and sold it for cash. They also sold other types of produce to the various markets in the city or peddled farm produce up and down the streets in residential neighborhoods.

It's kind of interesting that in those days, we separated the cream and took it to town and sold it for butter and fed the skim milk to the pigs. Today we separate it out and feed the skim milk to the humans, but I guess that's the way diets have changed.

Grandpa's favorite grocery store in Traverse City was Drew's Grocery, up in the Webster Street area on the east side of Traverse City. He sold his cream to the same creamery everybody else did, Tach's on State Street. His favorite thing to do was go to town and buy a ring of bologna before he came home. He loved store-bought bologna, so they usually ended up having bologna on Saturday nights after a day in town. (It may be that he was partial to bologna because he only had one tooth.)

Mary Frances (Limburger) Fromholz was actually born Catholic, but she left the church when she was sixteen years old. When she married my grandfather, who was Lutheran, she became a member of the Lutheran Church. My own mother did not join the Catholic Church until I was thirteen years old and in the eighth grade, while my German grandparents eventually joined the Methodist Church in Traverse City. They left the Lutheran church because they got mad at the minister for chastising the family at a funeral for not attending church regularly!

My grandmother inherited some money after her mother died, and with it she bought one of the original Milbert farms at the intersection of Garfield and Potter Roads. This was back in the early '30s, and she bought a team of horses and a piano and an automobile as well. She owned this farm and my grandfather owned his farm. When my great-grandparents deeded the Flanigan place to my grandfather, they would not allow my grandmother's name to be placed on the deed. I'm not exactly sure why, but they thought that was the thing to do. Therefore, when she bought her farm, she didn't place his name on the deed, and for years they each had their own farms. Grandpa farmed them both, but they kept separate records. I bring this up because there's a lot of talk nowadays about women's liberation, but I would make it absolutely clear that my grandmother was a liberated woman long before anybody else even thought of the term.

They kept accurate records of the crop production on each farm, and on the home farm Grandma owned the chickens. She bought feed for them from Grandpa and sold the eggs, and he rented her land to raise the feed on and so on back and forth. You can imagine how it would work out with two separate farm operations, but that's the way they conducted their business for many, many years. It wasn't until they were well into their 70s doing some estate planning that they finally joint-deeded the two pieces of property so they each held joint deeds on land that each had originally owned separately.

I had the pleasure of providing a tribute to my great-aunt Elizabeth (Fromholz) Dunn, the youngest daughter of Ferdinand and Johanna Fromholz and a sister to my grandfather, William Fromholz, upon the occasion of her one hundredth birthday. Aunt Lizzie had married John Dunn from a family west of Traverse City and they'd raised two daughters, Dorothy and Adeline. She lived most of her life in Lansing where Jack, as we called him, had half ownership in Toolens' Delicatessen over on Saginaw Street near St. Lawrence Hospital. That's significant, because when I attended Michigan State College and Clara was in nurse's training at St. Lawrence Hospital, we spent quite a bit of time with Uncle Jack and Aunt Lizzie. Clara was related through the Kratochvils to Jack Dunn and I was related, of course, to Elizabeth. They provided us with many Sunday dinners and transportation and lots of help when we were in those college days. Great-aunt Elizabeth retired in Texas and lived in an apartment in the senior citizens' housing and was still composing poetry well into her nineties. She was also a piano teacher in her younger days, and music stayed with her all those years.

The Kratochvils

I married Clara Belle Kratochvil from the Long Lake area of Grand Traverse County on August 16, 1949. She comes from a very old family in the area; they've been in the region one generation longer than mine. Her dad, Julius Kratochvil, was the son of Frank Kratochvil and Sadie (Sarah) McGarry. Frank in turn is the son of Wencil Kratochvil, the son of Franticek (Frank), who came into Traverse City in the 1850s from Chicago, emigrating from Androjov, a small village near Prague in the present Czech Republic. His first wife was a Wilhelm, another old family in the region.

Clara's mother was Ellen Courtade, the youngest of John N. Courtade's nine children, seven of whom were girls. The Courtades were farmers in East Bay Township in the Four Mile/Hammond Road area. John N. Courtade was the son of Peter Courtade, the son of Lorenz Courtade who came to Traverse City by way of Eagle Harbor on the Keewanaw Peninsula in the U.P. Just why that all transpired I've never dug into. John and his wife Luella (Schlosser) had two sons, Oscar and Peter, and then seven daughters, of whom Ellen was the youngest. The valedictorian of her class in 1923, she was quite well educated for her day and became a schoolteacher.

Clara has two brothers. Richard was at Michigan State the same time I was and graduated a veterinarian and practiced in the Traverse City area for many years. He married Jean Taylor from Newberry and they had five daughters. Her younger brother, Charlie, ended up on the home farm. He married Janet Wheelock and they had four daughters who are located in the area. Clara also has three sisters: Luella, who married Abbot Wilson, Eileen, who married Bob Milner, and Naomi, who married Jerry Benton.

My father-in-law used to tell the story that old Franticek, when he first got to Traverse City, couldn't speak any English, so one of his friends got him a job as a night watchman at a lumber mill. Perry Hannah, who owned the mill, lived up on Sixth Street. He used to get up at four o'clock in the morning to go down to the lumber yard to see whether the night watchman was on duty. Kratochvil caught him ducking around the lumber piles one night and grabbed him and put him into the little shack he stayed in on the property, holding him there until somebody came in the morning.

Hannah tried to explain that he was the boss, but he couldn't get Kratochvil to understand a word of English. Kratochvil held him until seven o'clock when the foreman showed up. When the foreman told him that was the boss and owner of the place, old Kratochvil started to apologize and Hannah said no, he was just exactly the kind of night watchman he wanted—somebody who would take care of things.

Hannah was also the founder of the Traverse City State Bank and my father-in-law used to borrow money there when he was buying cattle years ago. He always bragged to me that he could borrow money from the Traverse City State Bank because his great-grandfather had such a good reputation. Whether that's true or not, that's one of the stories they tell about old Franticek.

Franticek was initially married to a Wilhelm and they had several children, one of whom was Wencil Kratochvil. Wencil took up farming on Silver Lake Road near where the Carmelite Monastery is now. There used to be an old barn there on the south side of the road by the swamp and Wencil had a farm there. When Wencil's first wife died, he remarried and had some more children by his second wife.

One of the children of the first wife was Frank Kratochvil, Clara's grandfather. Frank bought the eighty acres about halfway between Silver Lake and Long Lake on Secor Road on the south side of the road. His brother Will had the farm down the road a half a mile or so to the west. Will eventually sold this farm to Clara's dad and this was where Clara was born and raised.

Frank Kratochvil, Clara's grandfather, married Sadie McGarry, whose father was Stephen McGarry. The McGarry farm was right across the road from the Frank Kratochvil farm on Secor Road. Clara's dad, Julius, used to tell the story that the Kratochvil farm on the south side of the road was on sandy enough soil that it originally grew pine, which could be logged and hauled to Traverse City for three dollars a thousand foot, so the Kratochvils were successful in making some money logging that land. Since the soil on the McGarry's farm on the north side of the road was heavier, they had elm and maple and hardwoods and there wasn't any market for it. All they could do was take down the trees and use them for firewood. In any event, both families cleared the land and farmed.

Old Steve McGarry, Clara's great-grandfather, was kind of an interesting person. He had been what they call a "hedgerow teacher" in Ireland. Since the British didn't allow schools for the Irish, kids were taught out in the fields behind the hedges. When Steve arrived in the United States in the 1840s, the only job he could find was joining the army and fighting in some of the Mexican wars. Steve McGarry was Catholic, but in his travels he met a young lady by the name of Umphries, an Orangeman from Northern Ireland who had come to the United States to make her fortune. She found out that Stephen McGarry could get a homestead of eighty acres as a result of having fought in the Mexican War, so they got married and she got him onto the farm and they cleared it up. Steve subsequently peddled geese and hogs and animals they raised in Traverse City.

One of the more interesting parts of Stephen McGarry's life was the fact that in the local school district, he was the interpreter. At school meetings, because the neighborhood consisted of the Bohemian Kratochvils, the German Herkners, and the French Campeaus and Secors, plus of course the Irish McGarrys, McGarry would interpret the information back and forth between the various languages.

Clara's dad, Julius, was a dignified, straight-laced gentleman. He was quite proud of his heritage, his family, and his own business abilities. He had a streak of humor once in a while. I remember him telling me about his neighbor, Mike Balzazak, a Polish farmer who lived south of him who had just come over from the old country. One day Mike came down to ask for help in rescuing a calf, probably a six hundred-pounder, that had gotten down into a pit alongside his barn. Clara's dad went over and sized up the situation. He had a sheepskin coat on and he unbuttoned it and all of a sudden jumped into the pit with a big roar. He waved that coat and the steer went right up on its hind legs and grabbed the top of the pit with its hooves and was out with no problem at all. He said Mike told him, "By Gott, Julius, you be smart man!"

Clara's dad was a pretty smart character in terms of how he handled his farming operation, but he had a tendency to be a little headstrong at times. I remember going out there one Sunday to ask for Clara's hand in marriage. Julius was in the living room reading the paper and I went in and told him I wanted to ask for his daughter's hand. It didn't make any difference whether he gave it or not, we were going to get married anyway, but I thought I'd like to ask.

He set his paper down momentarily and said that'd be fine with him, but warned me that he couldn't support two families. I was only eighteen, and I said, "You won't have to!"

A few years later, we were down at college. This was after Lisa and Molly were born and just before Peggy came. The fall before we hadn't made arrangements for housing, so we had to take a single trailer for a while. Clara had been telling her mother about it. My brother-in-law, Bob Milner, who's married to Clara's oldest sister Eileen (we've always been pretty close over the years), came to me and said the old man was telling the family he was going to have to help us out financially and arrange for our housing in Lansing. We were having Sunday dinner there and probably the subject would come up and he wanted me to be warned.

Sure enough, after dinner the old man invited me into the living room and said, "Now you go down to Lansing there and you pick out a house to live in .

I said no, I didn't think we needed that. I said I thought we'd get by just fine.

"Well," he said, "you don't need to think that anything I ever said to you when you wanted to get married—you don't need to worry about that."

I said, "No, I didn't."

We went ahead and lived in the trailer for a while until we got married housing at the university. We've thought about that offer several times since. You know, I'd probably have been smart to take his offer, but on the other hand, he gained a sizeable amount of respect for Clara and me because I didn't. In addition, she probably wouldn't have been happy if I'd done it. She was just like her dad in terms of having a mind of her own. So, finally, the old man got to where he'd ask my advice on lots of different activities in the business world and then we got along just fine.

Both sides of Clara's family were Catholic, but the Courtades were especially religious. I can remember when her granddad, John N. Courtade, died. I happened to be in the eighth grade at St. Francis. I didn't know Clara or any of her relatives at the time, but I had to go to the funeral because we were singing the Latin Mass. I remember the priest telling what a holy man John N. Courtade was. He'd been out to visit the farm one time and arrived after noon dinner and found John N. sitting under an apple tree saying his Rosary. I can recall hearing that story from 1943.

I said something to Clara's mother about it one time and she acted kind of surprised, but she saw to it that all her children got their instructions. However, she didn't send her older kids to St. Francis. The older two went to the public school and Clara started in the public school but for some reason decided to come over to St. Francis in the eleventh grade.

Her dad, at the time I went with her, was in the beef cattle business. He had accumulated about five hundred acres of land in Garfield and Long Lake Townships between Silver Lake and Long Lake, some of which was fairly heavy land and good for hay. The south end was a little bit light, but most of the land he accumulated was very good.

Originally he was in the business of milking short horn cattle. As a young girl, Clara milked cows and made hay and did all the things that had to be done on a dairy farm, but her dad decided he wanted to get out of the milk business and go into the beef business, so he set up a system of importing white-faced cattle (Herefords) from Montana to Traverse City. He would go to the areas around Izmey or Glendive, Montana, to get to know the ranchers. The Garber family from there still corresponds with us and we've been to their cattle ranch.

He decided he could make a living by bringing in 325- to 375-pound Herefords from Montana and putting them through the winter on hay and then pasturing them in the summer and getting them up to 650, possibly 700, pounds on roughage gain, without the use of grain, and then selling those 650- to 700-pound animals to feeders in the south part of Michigan that had great quantities of corn for fattening cattle. Utilizing roughage hay without having to put a lot of expense into it was a very good use of the land, and he made his living on the gain between 350 and 650 pounds or something in that range.

Julius pastured about 200 to 250 head of cattle on his own farms, but he also imported cattle for other farmers. He charged for buying the cattle and of course there were shipping charges back to Michigan. He also bought cattle for other farmers to the point that at one time he was bringing in a couple thousand head of cattle to our area. My own dad used to buy 125 cattle, and Clara and I had ten head of our own at one point when we were in college.

Julius' brother-in-law was Howard Arnold, married to Clara's mother's sister Bertha, and he also got into the business. They used to work together somewhat on it. Howard sold a lot to the feed-lot operators down south in the fall and took a commission for that.

At the time I got to know him, Clara's dad farmed with one small Ford tractor and a few other implements that he used for making hay and fixing fence, jobs they did on the farm. He carried on his cattle business all the time Clara and I went together and eventually sold it to his son, Charlie, when he reached sixty-five years of age.

Julius was also the director of the Farmers Mutual Insurance Company for many years, a local company in the Traverse City area put together by Clara's grandfather and several farmers, one of the first for mutuals in Michigan. Originally when they started, the group of farmers pledged to each other that if somebody's barn blew or burned down, they'd either build them a new barn or put up the money to do it and spread the risk. That eventually got translated into the mutual insurance company of which Julius became the director. He decided he wanted to get a license for selling insurance, so he did that also. From there he wanted to go into the real estate business, so he took the various courses and became an agent and then subsequently took the test for a brokers' license and became a broker, all in his late sixties. He had the Kratochvil Real Estate Agency until he finally retired.

Julius was a very astute businessman and a dignified gentleman. A Democrat, he ran for the House of Representatives from the Traverse City area in 1936. He didn't make it of course, as this particular area is heavily Republican, but he was pretty well known throughout the region. He could be a little bit intimidating if a person didn't know him, but he paid attention to business. He wasn't much of a drinker because he believed problems could come from the bottle, but he'd have a friendly schooner, as he would say, once in a great while. Clara's mother kept things pretty well organized in the house, so Clara comes from an industrious people and from a longstanding family in the Grand Traverse region.

As such, with her ancestors on both sides going back to the 1850s and 1860s in the region and my family on the Irish side going back to the 1860s and on the German side the 1880s, our children are some of the few of European descent in the Grand Traverse area whose ancestry on all sides goes back more than one hundred years.

Family Politics

My father was not always a Republican. Both my grandfathers were, but my father was a Democrat during my youth, even though there was always a minority of Democrats in Grand Traverse County and most definitely in Peninsula Township where he lived. He and his cousin Fred Carroll were two visible, outspoken Democrats in Peninsula Township at a time when it seemed everybody else was Republican. In truth, there must have been other Democrats, but not many. My father became a Republican about the time of Eisenhower's presidency.

I asked him one time why he was a Democrat. He said it went back to the early 1930s and the Great Depression. Though he was from an old established family in the township, he had so many brothers and sisters that he had to find employment as a hired man or work at some other kind of occupation in order to make a living before he was able to begin his own farm. He worked for various farmers on the peninsula, including George Bolling, Bert Bostwick, Clarence Anderson, Francis Hughes, and David Murray.

It was on the Murray farm that he met my mother. She was the oldest of a farm family of five children from East Bay Township, south of Traverse City, and she had come to the Murray farm to work in the household. My parents dated, went to dances together, and eventually married in 1929, but times grew pretty tough when the Great Depression hit. In 1935, my dad had an opportunity to buy the forty-five-acre home farm where I was raised on the peninsula, just north of the Chateau Grand Traverse winery on Carroll Hill on the opposite side of the road. He purchased it from my great-uncle Alfred McManus, better known as Uncle Alfie, who had bought the farm from Great-uncle George Carroll.

The first winter on the farm, my mother decided she wanted electric Christmas tree lights on the tree for my brother and me. She liked to do things like that and so she was after my dad to get electricity put in the house. When the Michigan Public Service Company, now Consumers Power, had first put the lines through on the peninsula, Uncle Alfie was tight enough that he hadn't signed up and instead used kerosene lamps for his source of light. I don't remember what the fee was to sign up, seven dollars or something like that, but Uncle Alfie wouldn't spend the money.

Since my mother wanted electricity, my dad went to town one Saturday and paid a visit to the Michigan Public Service Company office. A man by the name of Gage ran the place, Bert Gage, I think his name was. Dad went up to old Gage and told him who he was and that his wife, my mother, wanted electric lights for the kids for Christmas, so could he get hooked up for electricity?

Well, old Gage told him that the previous owner of that farm hadn't signed up when they went through, so in order to get hooked up today, there would be a fee of a hundred dollars. You can imagine that a hundred dollars in 1935 would be like ten thousand dollars today. A hundred dollars was the annual principal on the farm! My dad had to tell Gage he didn't have that kind of money.

Gage said, "I guess you don't get the electricity then."

My dad walked out with a dejected look on his face. Out on the sidewalk he bumped into old man Bolling, for whom he had worked at different times. George Bolling, who happened to be the chairman of the Democratic Party in Grand Traverse County, said to Dad, "What the hell's the matter with you, Mack? You're looking kind of down."

My dad said he was in town because Frieda wanted electricity so the boys could have lights on the tree at Christmas. He'd been in there talking to old Gage and Gage had told him he had to put up a hundred dollars to get the lights and he didn't have the money.

"Well," Bolling said, "you're in luck. Roosevelt down in Washington has just passed the REA (Rural Electrification Administration) bill and there's a clause in that bill that says if there's anybody who won't hook you up, you can take them to court and they lose their franchise. If you need any help," he added, "let me know."

My dad was an Irishman all the way and suddenly he had enough information to go back in and try again. He kind of cocked his hat on the other side of his head and walked right back up to old Gage and said, "I'm here to get some electricity."

Gage said, "Aren't you the one that was just in here and I told you you'd have to have a hundred dollars? Have you got the hundred dollars?"

The old man said, "No, I don't have it."

Gage said, "Then we're not going to be able to hook you up."

The old man said, "That's all I wanted to know. I was just out on the sidewalk talkin' to George Bolling, chairman of the Democratic Party in the county, and he was telling me that Roosevelt just passed some law that created REA and part of it says if you independent companies don't hook up somebody, you can lose your franchise."

Gage said, "And how soon did you say you wanted that electricity?"

The old man replied, "Just as quick as you can get your butt out there and get it hooked up!"

We had electricity by Christmas and Dad voted Democrat for years afterward, all the way through the '30s and '40s and '50s. He was a real fan of Franklin Delano Roosevelt. He finally voted Republican some after Eisenhower, but the whole thing went back to the attitude the Republicans had in 1935 and the way they treated people and the fact that Roosevelt would do something about it. Anyway, we had the electricity.

Chapter Two

Early Days on the Old Mission Peninsula

Recreational swimming has always been one of the uses of the bay, even though it doesn't warm up as quickly as some of the inland lakes. My grandmother told a story one time about deciding to go swimming with a girlfriend of hers. After they finished the noon dinner dishes one summer day up at the old house at the original Carroll homestead, they decided to walk to Willow Point, directly southeast about a mile, to a sand spit where they could swim.

When they ran out of the woods and onto the spit, they saw a sailing vessel pulled up alongside the shore. Sailors were running around stark naked while they washed their clothes in a big iron kettle on the beach with a fire under it. My grandmother and her girlfriend made a quick U-turn and headed back for the house at a dead run. They got quite a fright out of it.

A history of the McManuses of Old Mission would not be complete without a commentary on "Big Art" McManus. Big Art was a first cousin to my grandfather, Arthur McManus, known as "Little Art," and the son of Jim (James) McManus and his wife Hannah (Beattie) McManus. Hannah and Mary were sisters, so we had two brothers married to two sisters who came to the Old Mission Peninsula from the Dundee area, near Montreal, in Canada.

Uncle Jim, as he was affectionately called by Dad, though he was really his great-uncle, and Aunt Hannah raised their family north of where Bowers Harbor Park is today. Their son Art worked as a lumberjack in charge of various lumber crews and was famous throughout northern Michigan for his ability to fight. Many, many stories are told of Big Art. He had a habit in his younger days of going into Traverse City and having a few drinks in one of the local bars and then throwing everybody into the street, getting up on the bar, and dancing a jig. In those days, the polished-to-perfection hardwood counters were the pride of the owners, so they weren't too anxious to have Big Art dance on them,even though he would come back in on Monday morning and settle up the damages

Some of the owners bought him drinks to get him to stay off their bars, but one man decided to take other measures. Art always told the story that he walked into this particular bar one day and past the patrons sitting up on the stools. He came to an open place and ordered a drink. Just as he raised his glass, a fellow came past and bumped his elbow and spilled it. Art was a calm, cool, and collected individual who didn't lose his temper very easily, so he just ordered another drink. Just as he raised his glass, the same fellow came through and bumped his elbow from the other direction. Art looked at him and said, "If it's a fight you're lookin' for, there's no use spilling all this good whiskey!"

Right about that time, he found himself flat on the floor. He got up and went at the guy, but pretty soon he lit on the floor again. He found out this fellow was a pretty good scrapper, but one thing his opponent didn't know was that Big Art could fight with his feet just as well as he could with his fists.

As Big Art lay on the floor, he looked at his opponent and said to himself, "What you need is a damn good kick in the gut." He rose off his shoulders and let him have it. He knocked the guy down and gave him a few more punches 'till he got him squared away. Afterwards, he reported he didn't know 'till the end of the fight that the guy was a pugilist imported from Grand Rapids to give him a lickin'!

My dad always told another story about Big Art along the same lines. One time in the 1930s, Dad was hauling a load of fruit for Burkhardt Canning Company into the Upper Peninsula. They canned all kinds of fruit from the Grand Traverse region at their canning factory out on the peninsula, which was in our neighborhood: pears, peaches, applesauce, cherries. They even hired Indians to go up the Pine Plains, east of Traverse City near Arbutus Lake, to pick blackberries and blueberries and bring those to the cannery.

Burkhardt sold a lot of canned goods to the lumber camps, and Dad was driving a truckload into the Newberry area one day when they had a flat tire. In those days, they had to go to a blacksmith's shop to get the rim fixed. Dad was just a young fellow and he went in and the blacksmith asked who he was. He told him he was a McManus, George McManus from Traverse City.

A gray-bearded old gent was sitting over in the corner of the shop and he got up with tears in his eyes and said, "Who was your father?"

"Art McManus," Dad said.

The fellow said he knew an Art McManus who'd been foreman of the lumber camp up in the Newberry area many years before. Dad told him this must have been Big Art, a first cousin to my grandfather, and the old fellow proceeded to tell him a story about Art's days up in the Newberry area.

Big Art's fighting prowess was pretty well known to all the lumberjacks and people in the area, but one day a new fellow came into town and set up a bar and a brothel, or whorehouse as it was commonly called back then. He was a pretty good-sized fellow and a pretty good fighter himself, so he started to brag that he could lick anybody in the area, including McManus.

Eventually word got back to the lumber camp and was passed on up the line to Big Art. All the lumberjacks waited to see what he'd do, or perhaps more aptly put, waited to see when he was going to do it. One Sunday morning he said to the boys, "Hook up the team; we're going to town."

Everybody knew what was up, so they hooked up the team and all the lumberjacks in the camp rode with him. When they got to the edge of town, Big Art said, "Stop the team." He got out and walked down the center of the street, past the bar and whorehouse, and on down to the other end. Then he turned around. Of course, as he was coming back, the brothel owner came walking out and they went at it.

They had quite a scrap, and before long, most of the townspeople had gathered up and down the street to watch. Art said afterwards, "He damn near had me. He was a pretty good fighter. He had me down, but one of the whores cried out, 'It looks like you've got him!' and he turned his face. That was just enough for me to rise up off my shoulders and let him have it." Big Art had his caulked boots on from cutting timber and he went right to the side of the guy's head with one foot and then to the other side with the other and knocked him down and cleaned up on him good. That ended the scrap, and Art hooked up the team and went back to camp.

Big Art's physical prowess was well known in Traverse City as well. The story is told that when he was seventy years old, he could walk out of the barn in the morning with a pail of milk in each hand and still kick the lintel on the doorpost above his head with both feet and come back down without spilling a drop!

Big Art married Leticia Clune and they raised several children on their farm on the Old Mission Peninsula, one of whom, Alberta, was George Lardie's wife. Another daughter was Eva Crandall. In 1994, Eva was 102 years old and living in the Traverse City area. She had married Chum Crandall of Chum's Corner fame and they'd raised several children, including Curly and Max Crandall and Mrs. Ralph Zupin. Curly's daughter, Elizabeth Edwards Rollert, was a county commissioner in Grand Traverse County. Elizabeth also has a sister, so there are several descendants of Jim McManus in the Traverse City area. Young Max (Mickey) Crandall, who works at the bank, is another one.

Relatives also tell the story that Tish, as Leticia was known, got pretty mad at Big Art one day because when he and the hired man came in for dinner—they'd been out planting cherry trees that morning—the hired man looked like he hadn't taken a bath for a couple of days and was kind of shaken up. Tish wanted to know what had happened and Art said, "Oh, I tried to tell him how I wanted those trees planted and he didn't seem to get the idea, so I finally picked him up and stuck him headfirst into the hole, so I suppose that would kind of shake you up a little."

Another story about Big Art has to do with stumps. Whenever timber was first cleared on a farm, stumps were always left in the field that were gotten rid of over a period of time, but the first year or so after the timber was cleared, people just farmed around the stumps. Dad told me that Big Art was draggin' with a horse one day and got a little too close to a stump with the drag. He hollered "Whoa!" to the horse and reached down and picked the drag up and set it over a few feet so they could work around it. He was just that strong, a real bull of a man. I always figure he probably looked a lot like my cousin John Gallagher, who was built somewhat the same way.

Then there was the story of the murder of my great-uncle, Stephen Carroll. One day during WWII, my brother Frank and I were looking out the window when a 1934 Ford coupe drove into the yard. An elderly lady got out and I said, "Who's that?"

"That's Aunt Mame," Ma replied.

My brother Frank and I immediately began to wonder what was going to happen next, because we had been told for years that Aunt Mame was a witch and that she had been involved in the murder of her husband, Uncle Steve. She lived not more than a half mile from us on what is now known as Island View Road but in those days was called "the Swede Crossroad," so named because at one time a Swedish church stood near the west end on the north side of the road and many activities took place there for the Swedes in the neighborhood.

Our neighborhood was a mixture of Swedes and Irish, including the Bensons and Olsons and Larsons and Lyonses and Sundeens and Seabergs. C. F. O. (Carl Frederick Oscar) Nelson was one of the most famous of the group. They inter-neighbored with the Kellys and the Carrolls and the McManuses and the Buchans. Even though the Buchans are really one-half Scotch, they were still included with the Irish because old Grandma Buchan was a Carroll, so the Buchan tribe came from us and were at least half Irish.

Anyway, for years, even when we traveled the Swede Crossroad to visit other kids in the neighborhood, Frank and I had always avoided going near Aunt Mame's house, especially after dark.

Help was very difficult to come by at this time, as all the young men had gone off to war, and Aunt Mame was having trouble operating the farm she had inherited from her husband, my great-uncle. She had only one child by Steve, Cecilia, and she needed to have the cattle and horse manure taken out of the barn. She had come over to see my dad, her nephew by marriage, to find out if he would help clean out the barn, either for pay or for the manure, which could be used in his orchard. My father decided to help her out, but the guys he told to go help her were my brother and me! We had to go clean manure out of the witch's barn!

This caused us a great deal of consternation, but it wasn't the work that bothered us. I was fourteen and Frank was twelve and we were used to that kind of work. We had assisted many farmers in the neighborhood with spraying and harvesting fruit and different kinds of labor. The problem was, the lady of the house typically furnished you with noon dinner. In those days on the farm, you had three meals a day: breakfast in the morning, dinner at noon, and supper at night. Nowadays people talk about breakfast, lunch, and dinner, but in those days it was breakfast, dinner, and supper.

Frank and I decided we'd follow Dad's orders and go over and clean the barn, but one thing was for sure—we were not going to go in the house and eat anything Aunt Mame had cooked up! We informed our mother that we'd go over and work in the barn all morning, but we'd be home for dinner at noon and then go back, and that's exactly what we did. We just couldn't get past the story we'd been told.

Indeed, the story of the murder of Uncle Steve has been told many times in the region. The most recent version I'm acquainted with is by Larry Wakefield in the *Record Eagle*. He got part of it right, but his version isn't quite how the family tells it.

It seems that Stephen Carroll, my great-uncle, one of the sons of my great-grandfather Edward Carroll, was a very good fruit grower. He raised cherries and peaches and peddled his wares in Traverse City. For a farmer in his day, he did fairly well. He married Aunt Mame, whose maiden name I have never known, who had been married before to a man named Braddock with whom she'd had a son Jess, who also was brought up by Uncle Steve and Aunt Mame on the farm. At one point there were two kids on the farm, Jess Braddock and his half-sister Cecilia, who was a full cousin of mine. (There was also another Braddock sister who went to California after the murder.)

One morning in the 1920s when Jess was in his teens and in high school, they found Uncle Steve lying in the barn behind the horses, dead. They called the sheriff's department and the county coroner to come, and they concluded he'd been kicked in the head by the horses.

The neighbors didn't buy the story, because the team had never been known to kick. In fact, Uncle Alfie, who had driven the team many times, went right into the stall and sat down on the horses' hocks to prove to the sheriff that they'd never kicked Uncle Steve. Charley Lyons, a neighbor, also verified that the team didn't kick.

The family knew Steve and Jess had been in many arguments over money. Jess was a spendthrift who liked to pal around in Traverse City with some of the big guys and have a good time, and he was always trying to get money from Steve. The family suspected Jess had asked for money, or to borrow the car, and when Uncle Steve hadn't given it to him, an argument had followed that left Steve dead.

The family also believed Mame was an accomplice in the murder, based partly on circumstantial evidence: she had mopped the floor of the house at five o'clock in the morning, before breakfast, the morning Steve died, which the neighbors considered highly unusual.

A trial was held in Traverse City, but Jess had many friends among the sons of some of the higher potentates in town and the Carrolls didn't have much money with which to hire a good attorney. In the end, Jess was found not guilty, but the family always felt very strongly that Jess did kill Uncle Steve, and for years most of the family wouldn't speak to Mame or to Cecilia, her daughter, with the exception of Great-aunt Mabel's and Great-uncle Will's kids. Aunt Mabel never felt it was Cecilia's fault that her half-brother murdered Uncle Steve, so she instructed her kids to befriend Cecilia, which they did, and they protected her from the horse turds and stones thrown at her by the other cousins. As a result of that kindness, my cousin Raymond Carroll, Uncle Will's and Aunt Mabel's son, who at one time was supervisor of Peninsula Township, was able to buy Uncle Steve's farm from Cecilia and add it to his operation, as he was the only cousin she offered it to.

Clara and I lived in Aunt Mame's house for about three years when we graduated from college in 1953. By that time I had gotten over my concern about witchcraft, but the follow-up to the story is that Uncle Will and Uncle Andy, Steve's brothers, decided the year after the murder to go down to the fair in Cadillac, Michigan, to consult with a fortuneteller about finding the murder weapon. All the while, the neighbors had contended that someone had taken a horseshoe, then a hammer, and impressed the horseshoe on Uncle Steve's forehead. The trouble was, no one could find the hammer.

Uncle Will and Uncle Andy picked Cadillac because they were Catholic and it was against their religion to believe in fortunetelling. They figured if they went fifty miles away, nobody would find out about it, at least not until after the deed was done. So they went and consulted a fortuneteller and she described the neighborhood and scene to their satisfaction. She said if they went south and west of the barn, they'd find a ravine running from the Carroll farm down to the west arm of Grand Traverse Bay. At the bottom of the hill, they'd find a creek. (Incidentally, I think the creek actually begins on the John Lyons farm and flows at least part of the year down to the bay.) She said to follow that creek until they came to a bend where there was an elm tree standing and they'd find the murder weapon at the base of the tree.

The two returned to Traverse City and did what she said. They followed the ravine and found the elm tree. Lo and behold, at the base of the tree was a blood-stained hammer. In their minds, this proved conclusively that the Braddock kid had killed his stepfather, Uncle Steve.

The trial was over by this time and it was impossible to retry Jess, but knowing the trail he took when he left the murder scene the morning the body was found only added fodder to the fire: he walked along the country road that went along West Bay into Traverse City and eventually hitchhiked a ride from just south of Island View Road to town. Of course, if he were carrying the murder weapon, dropping it before he got to the road would have been logical. This convinced the family of his guilt, even if it was too late to convince the court.

In any event, after escaping conviction for his stepfather's murder, Jess was caught stealing gas and was shot at, losing one eye in the incident. He then took to robbing banks in Chicago, at which point the feds got after him. In the 1930s, Jess "fell" from an upper floor hotel window in Milwaukee, Wisconsin, and died. The family always said they never knew whether he jumped or was pushed!

The county was still pretty primitive in the late 1800s. When Alfred, Henry, Wilford, Arthur, and George were growing up, they got into a certain amount of deviltry like everyone else. One time they were at what is now Bowers Harbor Park and the Indians were camping there. In one of the tepees, a squaw had a porcupine underneath a crate. Wilford and my granddad were in the tepee and my granddad said he noticed Wilford looking over at the porcupine. He knew what he was going to do, so he got himself close to the door so he could get out of there fast.

Sure enough, Wilford turned that porcupine loose into the crowd of Indians gathered in the tepee and took off for home, about one-half to three-quarters of a mile to the south. A few braves took after them in hot pursuit. They had just about caught them when Wilford jumped up on a stump and took a broken tobacco pipe from his pocket. He pointed the broken pipe at the Indians and told them to go back. Because they thought the pipe was a gun, they did, and so the family survived the incident. This illustrates the fact that there were still Indians roving on the peninsula and holding powwows at Bowers Harbor at the time my granddad and great-uncles were growing up in the late 1800s.

At one time in the history of the original eighty acres Thomas Arthur and Mary bought, my great-grandfather's name was on the deed and Mary wanted my grandfather to have that land. Of her descendants, he had the only grandchildren carrying the name of McManus and she felt he had earned it and should have it. But the great-grandparents weren't getting along so well and the old man wasn't about to agree to that, so Mary took my grandfather into the bank in Traverse City, which I believe was probably the first People's Bank. They knew one of the officers and they had him set up the deed so that forty acres would go from Thomas Arthur to my granddad. The officer set the paperwork up and told my granddad to go ahead and sign his dad's name to the deed and then left the room while he did it. Eventually, my granddad gave twenty acres of the land to Verl, his oldest son. It had a good gravel pit on it and there was a lot of gravel hauled out of there over the years for roads on the peninsula. The other twenty acres went to the next boy, Harold Sr.

Granddad was kind of a tough old bird. He borrowed three hundred dollars one time from Will Buchan, his brother-in-law, and in turn Will put a mortgage on the eighty acres my grandparents lived on up on Carroll Road. Grandpa was raising "all them kids" (eleven) and having trouble making the interest, so he began getting behind in his payments. He heard that Buchan had sent the word out that he was going to foreclose on him and take the property. My grandmother was in tears and wanted to know what Granddad was going to do. He told her not to worry about it, that he'd take care of it.

Well, Buchan came over with his horse and buggy. Great-grand-dad Thomas Arthur was in the buggy with him. Buchan got out and told Grandpa he'd come to foreclose on the farm. My granddad's own father said to him in that conversation, "You know, Arthur, you have to pay your bills! If you're going to borrow money, you have to pay it back."

Granddad looked at Will and said, "Go ahead and foreclose if you want to, but if you do, it'll be the last piece of property you'll ever foreclose on 'cause you'll never have another chance." Buchan got

The second man from the right is A. T. McManus, grandfather of the author, flanked by sons Verl and Harold McManus. The blond boy in front is my father, George McManus Sr. Behind him is Ed Bopry, my 4-H leader. On the far left is Ed Bopry's father. Circa 1910

in his buggy and took Great-granddad back to the shore and didn't bother to file the papers because he knew my granddad meant exactly what he said.

Grandpa was tough in other ways, too. He always indicated that Verl got twenty acres off the original McManus piece and Harold got twenty. Harold then bought forty from Coolidges, who bought from Wilfred. The next three boys in line were each to get thirteen and a fraction off the home place to make up the back forty. They had been told they were going to get it and they assumed it was free and clear, but when they got to town to file the papers, Grandpa told them they'd have to cough up one hundred dollars a piece, because there was a three hundred-dollar mortgage on the farm. They did a little grumbling, but they each paid up and got their property.

One subject I haven't talked too much about is the matter of neighborhood feuds. The Hatfields and the McCoys down in the mountains of Kentucky and Tennessee are probably the most famous feuding families, but farm neighborhoods used to have a lot of petty feuds of one type or another.

The one I remember best is a situation that occurred out in Blair Township right after I moved out on Garfield Road in the 1950s. My neighbor, Donald Peart, came over to me one day with a little package. He opened it up and showed me a pink substance that had been a powder, but moisture had accumulated so it was more like a paste. He said, "What does this look like to you?"

I said, "It looks like lead arsenate, or arsenic of lead," which was a stomach poison that all the cherry farmers sprayed on their fruit as it began to turn color to control the cherry maggot, or cherry fruit fly. That insect was one of the few flies you could kill with a stomach poison. It fed off the surface of the leaves on the cherry tree, but in order to gather up the dust and other particles that might be food, it spit out some liquid from its siphoning proboscis and moisturized the surface of the leaf and then turned around and sucked up the moisture with whatever was in it. As such, you could kill that fly with a stomach poison and one of the most effective in the early days of spraying in the late '30s and early '40s was lead arsenate with its distinctive pink color. There wasn't anything else used on the farm that was colored like it, so there wasn't too much doubt as to what it was. Once in a while a cow was killed with the material because it apparently had a flavor that cattle liked and sometimes if farmers didn't dispose of their bags or containers that the material came in and a cow got loose, she'd chew on them until she got enough arsenic to kill her.

"Where'd you get it?" I asked.

He said he was filling silo over at the Strohm farm and was tending a filler and all of a sudden he noticed some of the corn stalks had this pasty pink substance swabbed on the tops of the ears. Usually if you had a fungus in the cornfield it was black, but this stuff was pink. He stopped the operation and brought a sample over for me look at, and then he took it to the police to be analyzed. Sure enough, it was arsenate of lead, so they went looking in the cornfield and found some of the material still swabbed on the tassel end of the ears. Without a doubt, somebody had come in during the night knowing they were going to fill the next day or so and swabbed on this lead arsenate. Since a limited number of people had the material available, one thing led to another and the police finally traced it to one of the neighbors and he finally owned up to it. Eventually they took him to court and he was fined.

Strohm got to thinking about it and began adding things up that had happened at his farm over the years, literally over a forty-year period. One time they had bought a prize bull and put it in the barn. When they came down to the barn one morning to do chores, the bull's tail was missing. Someone had come in and cut it off.

Another time they planted a new cherry orchard. When you plant a young cherry tree, you dig the hole and place the roots in the hole and then stamp the dirt good and tight around the roots so that as they begin to grow, they'll be able to obtain moisture and nutrients from the soil. One thing you don't want in the root area is air pockets. Well, the Strohms had planted a young cherry orchard, and a few days later, Bill just happened to notice something wrong with the trees. He got to investigating and found someone had come along and pulled the trees up about three or four inches to create an air pocket under them. Luckily, they were able to put the trees back in and stamp the dirt around them. Again, they couldn't figure out who had done it, but once the lead arsenate problem was traced, they knew immediately who had been doing all these things over this lengthy period. As they added it up, apparently it had been over a piece of property the Strohms had obtained that the other neighbor had wanted to buy.

I got to talking to Father Kohler down at St. Francis in Traverse City one day and he said that in Europe, in the old days, feuds between neighbors were common. It used to be something the ministry regularly had to deal with and apparently it carried over when some of those immigrants came to the United States. I don't think it's probably out of the question today.

In 1940, my fifth grade year, we moved up to the Anderson farm just north of McKinley Road. Clarence Anderson was the manager of Traverse City and he had inherited a farm from his mother, Mrs. Bard. He had a cherry orchard there and my dad had worked for him at different times. Clarence asked my dad to take care of the orchard the following summer and Dad decided we needed to live in the Anderson house for a part of the year for some reason I'm not exactly sure of. The house was back off the road a ways. The farm was later owned by Leslie Jamieson and is just north of what used to be the Underwood Farm and before that the Titus place on McKinley Road.

At the time we moved there, Center Road was a gravel road, but they decided to pave the first portion from Traverse City north. For some reason, the end of the pavement ended at the north end of Anderson's farm. I don't know whether that had anything to do with the fact that he was the city manager, but that's as far as the pavement came the first time they paved the gravel on the peninsula.

Speaking of Center Road, why was it made a state highway and the name changed to M-37? As far as I'm concerned, there's no good reason M-37 is a state highway. It's a spur of the state highway system from Front Street in Traverse City to the lighthouse at the tip of the Old Mission Peninsula, so it's basically a dead end (one of those places you can't get here from there). My father, who worked for the state highway department that cared for the state roads before they were taken over by the counties in the 1940s, always claimed that designating Center Road M-37 and making it part of the state highway system (with subsequent monetary compensation) was a political decision.

Dad and I talked about this and more those times I rode the snowplow with him from our house to the end of the peninsula and back to keep him awake during big snowstorms. He felt that Murray D.

VanWagoner, the state highway commissioner running for governor as a democrat back in the 1940s, thought he could pick up a few votes by making it a state highway. He lost, and Dad's comment (he was a Democrat at the time) was that peninsula voters voted the same (Republican) after or before, so it didn't do him any good.

There would be some justification to having the road a state highway if the state property near the lighthouse were designated a state park and advertised as such. However, the opposition to such a move (thanks to traffic) was so great that the DNR essentially gave the operation of the property over to the peninsula government with the proviso that anyone could use it as long as they followed the rules laid down by the peninsula. Needless to say, promotion for widespread state road use is minimal! Nonetheless, the mileage on the peninsula spur of M-37 has provided the Grand Traverse County Road Commission with state operation and capital dollars since the designation.

Anyway, back when their kids were growing up, in order to make cash, Grandpa McManus worked in the logging camps, usually in the Alba or Mancelona areas, and came home on the weekends on the train. One weekend he returned home to find Grandma in tears. She was having problems with Verl and Harold. They had been into a little typical deviltry that young boys get into and had tipped over somebody's corn shocks. A couple of her sisters-in-law, Aunt Lil and Aunt Daisy, had told her that if those boys didn't straighten up, they would have to go to reform school. Grandma was pretty upset that her sisters-in-law would put her boys in reform school and so she was crying on my granddad's shoulder about how tough things were.

He wanted to know who the ringleader was and Grandma told him it was Aunt Lil. Well, Granddad never did get along all that well with Aunt Lil. She tended to be kind of a character. One thing about her was she was a damn poor euchre player. My grandpa was a good euchre player, and when you play euchre, if you've got the right bower you lead it, and if you've got the left bower you lead that too, right along behind it. One of the worst things you can do is hold the bowers until the last two tricks, and that's exactly what Aunt Lil tended to do. In those days they had neighborhood card parties and they traded partners. My grandpa, who liked to win, always had to bite his tongue when he got Aunt Lil for a partner because he knew damn well that if she had the bowers, she's hang onto them until the last dog was hung, and you can't win that way.

Grandpa also had a great affinity for remembering everything that had ever happened in the neighborhood. Both my grandpas were good at that. In fact, they kept track of what everybody had done practically from the time they were born, especially if they'd done anything that wasn't quite on the up and up. Grandpa had the goods on Aunt Lil, so he told my grandma not to worry and that he'd take care of it. Well, whenever my grandpa said he'd take care of something, you knew it was time to stop the conversation. It might take him a day or two, but he followed the old adage, "Don't get mad; just get even."

He knew they were having a neighborhood card party Saturday night, and he waited until he got Aunt Lil as a partner in the euchre game with everybody sitting around. There kind of came a lull in the conversation, so he could be heard without raising his voice too much, and he looked across the table and said to Aunt Lil, "Do you mind the time your father caught you and one of the neighbor boys in the toilet together?" Well, Aunt Lil's face got kind of red and we never heard any more about reform school!

My father, George McManus, had a sense of social justice that I have not seen equaled in many others. We were very poor people in the 1930s at the height of the depression, with no money and very little to make due with, but we were employed at least periodically(one winter at two dollars per week) and were working to build the orchards and we also had cows, chickens, and pigs enough that we had food to eat. But my father had a cousin who lived on Blue Water Road, east of the Catholic Church, about one-half mile. She was the daughter of Aunt Kate (Carroll) Bucere. I believe she had some half-brothers and sisters, but we'll have to find that out another time. As far as I know, she was the only child of Aunt Kate with Bucere, but that may not be the whole story either.

I remember I was a very small child—it must have been prior to 1938, because I don't think my sister Antoinette was born yet—when my father got the word that his cousin was in serious trouble. She had a big family. I don't remember exactly how many children there were at the time, but it seems to me there were five or six or seven, maybe more, and they were very poor. Her husband had trouble finding work, and word came to my dad that she was down in bed with a new baby and she had milk fever. One breast had swelled to the size of a milk pail. Her husband was off looking for work and she needed help.

I remember going down to their farm, if you can call it that. The house was old and dilapidated and we went in and there she was in bed, sick. It seemed like there were kids all over the place, dirty dishes, and the floor hadn't been swept, mopped, or cleaned in a long time. It was probably one of the most poverty-stricken situations I've ever seen.

I remember one of the boys only had two fingers on his hands and that impressed me. I inquired as to what had happened and they said he'd been playing with some dynamite caps he'd found, probably on the Mert Gilmore farm. The boys had gone down to the beach and put a dynamite cap on the stone and hit it with another stone to make it go off. In the process, young Mitch had gotten his thumb and a couple of fingers blown off.

His mother was in a real dilemma. The baby was crying and one of the little kids was trying to feed it cold milk from the cow they kept. I know my mother helped them get the bottle heated up. We took a couple of the kids and the baby up to our house for a few days to help out.

While we were there, Dad asked his cousin if she'd tried to get help from the church. Some of her uncles were pillars in the Catholic Church in Mapleton. She indicated that she hadn't, but none of them had come around to offer, either. Then he asked if she'd been to welfare. Now Dad hated the social welfare system with a passion. He would never, even in the height of the depression, take the least bit of welfare assistance, but he realized that in her case, the time had come to seek help. She told him she had gone in, but they wouldn't give her any assistance unless she agreed to be sterilized. This infuriated my father, who was a great believer in families.

At home, he stewed about it for a couple of days. Finally he said to my mother, "We've got to do something about this situation."

Mother said, "What are you going to do?"

He said, "Get in the car. We're going to Elk Rapids to see the priest." We didn't have money to waste on gas, but this was something that had to be done, so we got into our Ford Model A and drove to Elk Rapids and Dad told the priest that a parishioner over at the mission in

Mapleton was in sad need and nobody was doing anything about it. No local help was available and she had been to the social welfare department and they wouldn't give her any help unless she was sterilized.

That got the priest going and he said, "Come on. We'll go down and see about that."

They drove into Traverse City and went to the office of the social bureaucrat in charge, who repeated to the priest that he wouldn't give her any help unless she'd sign a form to be sterilized.

My father said the priest's face got about the color of chalk, and then he reached out and grabbed the bureaucrat by the shirt and necktie and fetched him up out of his chair until they were nose to nose and he said in a loud voice, "The woman needs help and she needs it *now*." Then he set him back down. The bureaucrat got the papers out to provide help without further comment. One thing Dad couldn't stand was bureaucratic potentates who acted like little dictators. The priest did his job, and we always respected him for it afterwards.

The family eventually moved to Detroit and got work and raised a large family. I don't know how many of them there were, but I think eight or ten, and as far as I know they've all been gainfully employed. One of them ended up with a set of cabins and a bar almost up to Paradise in the U.P. My brother Frank and my dad visited them over the years, and they used to stop into the home farm when they came to Traverse City, as they had a great love for my dad for taking care of a bad situation and seeing to it that the bureaucrats didn't have their way.

I saw my dad act on other occasions when people needed help, too. We had a Mexican cherry picker one time in the 1940s. He was one of the first Mexicans from Texas and was an American citizen. The man's wife was going to have a baby and they didn't have money for her to deliver in the hospital. In those days, Grand Traverse County ran a county hospital for indigents, but you had to be a resident of the county in order to get any help; otherwise you were turned away. Dad thought there ought to be a way to get the woman into that hospital so she could deliver the baby there.

The cherry picker was a pretty sharp Mexican. He knew what was going on. He could talk English all right, but my dad told him when they went in to talk to the bureaucrat that he should play dumb and let him do the talking.

They went in and of course the bureaucrat got the paperwork out and started on the usual questions. Dad said the Mexican played it out the best he'd ever seen. He acted like he was the dumbest man ever born. He didn't know where he was from or what he was up to or practically his own name. Finally the bureaucrat gave up and admitted his wife to the county hospital and his wife had the baby and everything turned out just fine and nobody was the worse for it.

Depression times were tough, tough, tough, financially. My dad said one time he said to his dad "this generation will never stand for it." His dad replied, "Oh yes they will, just like we stood for the panic of '98 (1898)."

Chapter Three
Local Communication and a Little Local Culture

We got our first phone back in the 1940s. It hung on the wall and had a crank on the side; our number was 14F2. There were eight people on our line on the north end of the peninsula. You could crank whatever number on your line you wanted, and the people could pick up the earphone and you could talk. If you wanted somebody on another line, you pushed a button on the side of the phone and cranked it and then you got the operator, who would connect you with the number you wanted on another line.

We lived just to the north of the line between the Traverse City phone exchange and the Mapleton exchange, so we were always on the Mapleton line. It was a long distance call for many years to call our neighbors on the other side of the hill. We weren't allowed to waste money that way, and very few long distance calls were ever made from our place.

Living in the country as we did, the phone was an important source of news. Whenever your phone rang, when you picked up the receiver, you could usually hear two or three or four clicks on the line as neighbors who didn't have too much to do at that time of day picked up and listened in. That used to be pretty common, and anything you said on the telephone, you could be pretty sure the neighbors knew all about it.

The other unique thing in those days was that the phone was also the fire alarm. If there was any kind of brush fire or house or barn fire on that end of the peninsula, you transmitted the news to the telephone operator at Mapleton and she would put one long ring on each of the lines and everybody would pick up the receiver on their particular line and she would tell them where the fire was. Of course, the neighbors all turned out to fight the fire. In the summertime and in the fall and spring, before the weather froze up, farmers kept their spray machine tanks full of water. In case of a fire, all they had to do was hook up a tractor—I don't remember doing it when we had the horse-drawn sprayer, but I suppose they did it in those days, too—and go help. Quite often the fires were brush fires, started when a grower was burning brush and the fire got away and spread into dry grass.

Out of that system emerged the volunteer fire department on the peninsula, which is a very important asset to the community from many standpoints. Out of that emerged the first fire hall or fire barn on the peninsula, just north of Mapleton. After that, a second fire barn went up at the south end of the peninsula, but the old wall telephone that operated with a crank was a very important communication piece when I was a boy.

It was quite a bit of progress when eventually the phone system was connected to Traverse City in such a way that you didn't have to pay long distance from Mapleton to Traverse and the north half of the peninsula no longer had to pay long distance to talk to the south half. The Peninsula Telephone Company has continued to operate under the able management of Jack Solomonson and his wife Vi, and Jack has been not only a very able manager, he's been a strong political figure statewide in the independent telephone company movement.

As I recall, when I was growing up, Arnie White ran the Peninsula Telephone Company and it was he and his wife Loretta and Mrs. Wood and some of her daughters who were operators of the phone company. Mrs. White and Mrs. Wood were sisters, Emery girls from Bowers Harbor, and the phone exchange was located in a house just north of Mapleton.

The newspaper was available when I was growing up, but not always in the rural areas, and not everyone took the local paper. I remember that my great-uncles Will and Andy Carroll who had the two farms just north of us subscribed to the *Grand Rapids Press*. They bought one paper a day and first one family read the paper and then they took it over to the other family to read.

Radio was not common at all. There were no TVs, no fax machines, no Internet, and no information highway. There wasn't even a radio on most farms, but my dad bought a radio in the late 1930s and he liked to listen to the prize fights with Joe Louis or Billy Conn. Later on we also listened to the voice of Harry Heilmann as he announced the Detroit Tigers.

We had a neighbor come up one night to listen to a prize fight, probably between Joe Louis and Billy Conn. Pretty soon the neighbor said to my dad, "By golly, George, that's a fast fight or else your radio plays faster than mine!"

It was a big addition to farm life to have a radio. I can remember on the eighth of December in 1941, the day after the Japanese attacked Pearl Harbor, Mrs. Pitcher, our teacher at the Maple Grove School, brought a radio to school. That was the first time we'd ever had a radio in school. She wanted us to listen to the news about the war and what the Japanese were doing to us in the Pacific.

We didn't have a radio station in Traverse City until about 1939. Prior to that time we listed to WGN out of Chicago. We could get this station best at night, and another station carried the Renfro Valley Boys out of Tennessee on Saturday nights.

During World War II, the major radio announcer was Gabriel Heatter. During World War II, we listened to Gabriel Heatter and his "Good News Tonight" (or bad news tonight) at six o'clock as we ate supper.

Les Biederman came to Traverse City from Pennsylvania in the late 1930s. He got the charter to establish WTCM, the first radio station in Traverse City. It was a big innovation to have a local station and Les was a colorful character. He had a million ideas about the way the world ought to run and what the country needed, so he not only brought in the radio, he became an active member of the community.

He also editorialized in later years on the radio on a host of subjects. He wasn't exactly a Rush Limbaugh, but he did have an opinion on many things and a lot of them were for the good of the community. He was an especially heavy supporter of Northwestern Michigan College and prided himself on being one of its founders, although the real originator was Glenn Loomis, the superintendent of schools. Several others worked hard to get the college, too, but Les was always the outstanding figure because he had the media at his command, at least the radio media, and he was dedicated, plus he insisted it be a community college rather than a junior college that Loomis promoted.

There was quite a lot of competition in those days between WTCM and the *Record Eagle* in terms of who was going to get the advertising dollar and who was going to get the editorial command of the community. John Anderson worked for Les in those early days, but he broke off from WTCM to found the second radio station in Traverse City, WCCW. The number of radio stations in Traverse City has proliferated considerably since that time.

Les could see that television was going to come onto the scene, so he eventually formed WPBN TV, now Channel 7 and 4. Prior to that, the first television we had in northwestern Michigan was WWTV Cadillac. You could get that signal with rabbit ears if you lived on top of a hill. Otherwise, you had to put an antennae on top of your house or on some kind of pole in order to get sufficient height to pick up the television signal from Cadillac.

The *Record Eagle* was a combination of a couple of local papers that had been in the Traverse City area for many, many years. At the time I was growing up, the Batdorffs owned the paper and Jay Smith was the editor. Jay used to write the editorial column and usually had another column with some of his own philosophies about the area. He was followed by his son, Bill Smith, and Austin Batdorff was followed by his son. During the time the Smiths and Batdorffs had the *Record Eagle*, it was a local paper and carried local items of interest much more than it does today. It was considered to be an accurate source of information and one that portrayed many of the good things in the community.

Later on, the Batdorffs sold the paper to a chain of newspapers and it took on a definite eastern establishment flavor. There is quite a difference in the paper today as contrasted to the Batdorff and Smith days.

The radio station, WTCM, has the distinction of carrying the oldest continuous farm program in the state of Michigan. When Biederman came in, he got acquainted right away with Carl Hemstreet, the county agricultural agent, and he and Carl put together a farm program that took place during the noon hour every day. In the early days the program was longer than fifteen minutes, more like a half hour, and provided Extension information from Michigan State University and from other sources that would benefit farmers in the community and also homemakers and 4-H people, students and boys and girls in the 4-H program.

The original program involved an agricultural agent, a "home demonstration" agent, and a 4-H agent in kind of a three-way conversation about information and improvements that farmers and their wives and children could make. Back then, Edna Deo, later Edna Alsup, was the home demonstration agent, and Andy Olson was the 4-H agent. Eventually Hemstreet became the horticultural agent for northwestern Michigan and Arthur Glidden was brought in from Gaylord to be the county agricultural agent. Then the style of the program began to change and each agent took a turn hosting the program, but it was heavily oriented to Glidden and Hemstreet talking about agricultural and horticultural practices.

The program had a huge listenership in the rural communities, especially during the spring and the rest of the growing season, when people in the fruit business were looking for information about when to spray.

One story goes that Bill Wilson on the peninsula was in such a hurry to get in from the orchard one day to hear the program that he went around the barn a little too fast with his tractor and sprayer, cutting the corner a little too closely and tearing the spray boom off the spray machine. Everyone got quite a hoot out of how Bill was in such a hurry to get the latest information on what to spray that he broke his spray machine getting to the radio! Bill wrote a poem I've always enjoyed that pretty much tells it like it is when it comes to fruit farming.

Setting Out an Orchard

When you look upon a sleet storm, a' glistening in the sun,

Can you see the beauty, and not the damage done?

When the mercury's down to zero, then drops twenty more
    degrees,
Can you think of pretty penguins, and not about your trees?

On a nippy, frosty morning, when spring is in full flood,
Can you go about your morning chores and never cut a bud?

When your cherry crop needs picking and the crew all heads for
    town,
Can you wish them pleasant going, and not let it get you down?

If a thunderhead looms up as the summer sun grows pale,
Can you think of Benny Franklin, and never once of hail?

When things like these turn up, if your mind will not be tortured,
Then go ahead and stake the ground and plant your cherry
    orchard.

—Willard (Bill) Wilson   Wilson Road   Peninsula Township

I came on the scene in 1956 as marketing agent on a district basis for MSU Extension. I was no sooner on the job when Art Glidden said to me, "Now it's time for you to take your turn on the radio. I'll get you introduced and we'll do a program today while we're there." It was just a couple of blocks up to the radio station from my office at the post office, although the station wasn't always located where it is today. Originally it was downtown on Front Street. I remember saying to Glidden as we left the office, "What are we going to talk about?"

He replied, "We'll worry about that when we get there."

Art was always a very philosophical sort of guy, and he covered the weather first and then led into the discussion topic. After he introduced me, I made my first comments and we did the program. Art had in his head what he wanted to say before we went over there, but he gave little warning and tended to fly by the seat of his pants.

Hemstreet had been killed in an accident prior to my joining the Extension service, and he was replaced by Clarence Mullet from Newaygo County, who'd been the county agricultural agent. There was also a consumer marketing agent at the time named Ruth Hunsberger. She was part of a program designed to take care of the agricultural food information in terms of the consumer. Her husband was judge of probate for many years and her son Art ended up one of the high school principals in Traverse City.

When Mullet retired, I was made the Horticultural and Marketing agent. When Glidden retired, I was appointed the CountyExtension Director, which was the new term for the county agricultural agent. This was in 1968, and the horticultural agent's position wasn't replaced until Dr. Charles Kesner came along about a year later.

During that year I had five radio programs a week to do, plus other media. We did some writing for the paper and periodically some television as well. It was a little more media than I cared to be involved in, so I split it up with the home agent and the 4-H agent. I also began to encourage other county extension directors in the five-county area around Traverse City (Stanley Ball in Leelanau County, Charlie Twigg in Benzie County, Walter Kirkpatrick in Antrim, and a succession of agents in Kalkaska County, including Warren Cook, Norm Brown, Reuben Kaarre, Ben Porter, and different agents) to take the program once in a while. We also split it up some with the U.S.D.A. people. Guy Springer and Virgil Thayer were in the U.S. Soil Conservation Service and we also had help from the Farmers Home Administration with Phil French and then the Agricultural Stabilization Committee, which was eventually run by Lowell Goff.

I probably had one of the original call-in radio shows when I began calling in to do the show instead of going back to the station. Merlin Dumbrille, the announcer for many, many years, worked very well with the extension agents and others who conducted the program. He said to me one day, "If you're out in the country, why don't you just call in and we'll talk over the telephone?"

This was a good attention-getter for farmers. Wherever I was, Merlin would indicate that I was on so and so's farm today. Quite often another farmer would come over or meet me somewhere along the road to fill me in on something on his farm that he wanted me to look at and provide advice about.

We also eventually began to tape the program ahead of time so the radio always had programs to run, even if we were going to be elsewhere such as in East Lansing for meetings or this and that.

Working on the radio was a good experience. I did it for twenty-five years in extension and I also did it while in the legislature. My first television appearance was live, on WWTV Cadillac, in 1956 or 1957, when Mrs. Hunsberger, the consumer marketing agent, asked me to do a show with her about the cherry industry.

I've done many, many television appearances since that time, but none of us ever had any real training for it. I was a college graduate horticulturalist with an agricultural economics minor and I simply knew the kinds of things we needed to talk about. We'd had communications courses and speaking and writing in college and also a certain amount in high school, so we could put two and two together. But as far as any particular training on how to conduct a radio or television program went, we learned that on the job. The main thing was to have a message that could be understood by a majority of the people and to get it done in the time allowed.

At the same time, you couldn't have the subject run out too quickly so that you had thirty seconds or one-minute pauses where nothing was said. If you had five minutes to fill, you'd better have five minutes' worth of something to say, and what you needed to say had to be important to people and in words they could understand.

One of the unfortunate aspects of television, and it's also true of radio to a certain extent, is it causes us to encapsulate ideas into short "sound bites"—little short squibs geared to capture an idea and get it across to people. This limits any thorough discussion of an issue. Quite simply, a lot of issues in life aren't so black and white. Usually—hopefully—the speakers have thought through all the ramifications and those sound bites are a result of a lot of soul-searching, but such a short segment still limits the discussion of an issue as a whole.

Our society just plain moves faster today than it did fifty years ago. It seems as though people had more time when I was growing up to thoroughly discuss a concept or piece of new information. Farmers had a notorious ability to do that. My dad could talk for an hour or two with his closest friend, Cal Kelly, and he periodically stopped by to visit with his mother and discuss issues of one sort or another with her, whether it had to do with family or politics or something going on in the community. Back then there was more time and fewer subjects.

It's interesting that the Michigan legislature moved to M-Span (live TV). My first reaction is that it will lengthen the amount of time it's going to take to get anything done, because it's probably going to encourage a lot of legislators who previously might have voted on an issue but not spoken on it if someone else had already covered it fairly well. If we have television cameras viewing the daily proceedings of the legislature, it might become imperative that everybody get up and make a speech once a day or so, and if you multiply that times thirty-eight in the Senate and 110 times in the House . . . Well, at least I hope they'll keep the speeches fairly short.

The up side of putting the workings of the legislature on TV is that those people who care to watch will be up to date on exactly how things are going. I don't know whether or not they're going to put M-Span in the governor's office, but in terms of the other two houses, the information is readily available.

I always enjoy watching C-Span. It's interesting to see federal legislators standing in front of the mike with most the seats in the chamber completely empty, blazing away about an issue. It's also interesting to see other legislators come down the aisle and walk behind the speaker looking very intent and busy. It always occurs to me that they could go around the back of the room so as not to step in front of the television, but apparently they want a little free exposure on national TV.

To sum up the media in terms of the people who listen, read, and watch, probably the best advice is to only believe half of what you see, a third of what you read, and a quarter of what you hear!

The Traverse City State Hospital

The Traverse City State Hospital, also known as the Regional Psychiatric Hospital or simply "the asylum," used to play a very important role in the lives of the people in the Grand Traverse region who were employed there. It was one of the largest employers in Traverse City for many years, not only of townspeople, but of many farmers as well. The farm boys could put in eight hours working in the hospital and still work on the farm after hours and on weekends; oftentimes they would milk the cows before they went to work in the morning. Many of them started their own farms as individual entrepreneurs and still worked at the state hospital. Fred Coolidge, my dad's first cousin and one of our neighbors, was one of the peninsula farmers who worked at the state hospital.

The hospital is closed now and the place has been dressed up; it's now called the Grand Traverse Commons. Likewise, the creek that flows through the east side of the property that was always known as Asylum Creek has since been upgraded to Kids Creek. For us old-timers, the state hospital provided not only a source of employment but lots of conversation. People always talked about the many things that happened there, as well as speculated about things purported to have happened there.

At about the seventh grade level, school children used to be taken on a tour of the hospital. I remember going through and seeing various patients and experiencing some of the hollering and yelling. I guess we always learn lessons, no matter what spot we're in, and the state hospital taught me a couple that were kind of interesting.

The hospital, at one time, raised most of the food the patients ate. The grounds contained vegetable gardens, fruit orchards, animals, and a very high class premium Holstein dairy herd. It was always called "the state herd" and it was always exhibited at the Northwestern Michigan Fair in Traverse City back when the fair was located where the Civic Center is now on East Front Street. The patients always came down to the fair and took care of the animals, milked the cows, and so on.

In addition to the feed the hospital raised, they bought a lot of hay from surrounding farmers. When I was in my teens, my dad used to haul hay to the hospital. We didn't raise hay on our farm, but we bought hay down in the Missaukee County/McBain area as well as other places like Falmouth, south of Cadillac, and then we turned around and sold it to the state and delivered it to the hospital.

I remember one time we took a load in and backed the truck into the barn with a load of baled hay on top. About a half dozen patients jumped up on the load to help and I jumped on too. When you're handling baled hay, you use a J-shaped hook with a sharp end in order to grab the bales and it can be a rather dangerous weapon. I remember my dad saying to me, "Get the hell down off that load and get out of there. Them patients know what they're going to do, but you don't know what they're going to do."

That lesson stuck with me for a long time. Lots of times when I get into a group that acts about the same as those patients at the state hospital in terms of the way they're going at the solution to a problem, I always think of that. It's probably a good time to get the hell out of there. They may know what they're doing, but nobody else does.

My dad also taught me another important lesson from the state hospital. As a young lad, like all young people who have a little education, I started thinking I knew more about the rest of the world than the rest of the world did. I was in one of those kinds of moods one day when I was talking with my dad, so he put me in the car and we drove up past the state hospital. He said, "You see that hospital over there? Them people in there think everybody else on the outside is crazy."

Well, I always remembered that. Sometimes if you think maybe the rest of the world doesn't understand just exactly what you're doing, they probably think you don't understand either.

A scientific discovery that happened at the state hospital that's frequently overlooked today is the discovery of the importance of cobalt as a trace mineral in animal feed. The Traverse City State Hospital was where the importance of trace minerals to the cows' diet was discovered. The soil at the hospital lacked that particular element, so no matter how much the cows ate, they lost weight because they didn't have the trace mineral needed to digest their feed. In some of the old animal husbandry publications I studied when I was in college, I read a description of the disease. The cure was just to add the trace mineral to the animals' salt. This was a very simple but important discovery, and it happened at the Traverse City State Hospital. For many years it was labeled "Traverse City Disease"before the nutrition aspect was discovered.

Many stories used to circulate about things that happened at the hospital. Because of what we heard about electric shock treatments and other kinds of treatments for the mentally ill, nobody ever wanted to have to go there. It was a place to be feared and avoided unless you worked there, but some of the more daring young ones used to venture onto the grounds and even into the buildings to see what they could get away with.

Probably one of the most innovative and interesting events that happened in the life of the hospital was the development of the Traverse City State Hospital All Faiths Chapel. I believe it's the only place I've ever seen where one end of the church is Catholic, the other end of the church is Protestant, and the middle is Jewish on one side with offices on the other side. There were three faces, so to speak, in the same building, and the priest, minister, and rabbi worked together to serve the patients. The chapel was open to the general public and a number of people in Traverse City and the surrounding area attended services there on occasion. Some of them attended quite regularly, rather than attending their own parish or church.

Father Frederick came along as pastor of the Catholic end of the All Faiths Chapel following World War II. He meant a lot to many people in the area. When the state hospital was finally closed, he moved into parish work in the region, but he continued many of the activities he had begun when working at the All Faiths Chapel. He eventually formed the Father Fred Foundation, which collects money, groceries, clothing, and so on for the poor. Some of the former state hospital patients who stayed in the area were often in need and Father Fred tried to take care of them, and he also took care of a lot of other people in the community. To accomplish this charitable work, he operated out of St. Joseph's Catholic Church in Mapleton and managed the Father Fred Foundation out of Traverse City.

The chapel was built with private donations from people in the Traverse City area. When the state hospital closed, the state gave the chapel back to the community by way of the Women's Resource Center, intended for victims of domestic violence. The superintendent's house, which is south of the chapel, was given to the Women's Resource Center at the same time as a home for victims of domestic violence. The chapel was also used for offices. Then it was sublet to some children's organizations, so it was put to good use even though it was no longer used as a chapel.

When the state gave the hospital back to the community in 1990, the roof leaked quite badly, so it was imperative that it be transferred to the community in order to be fixed. This happened my first term in the state Senate, and I was instrumental in getting those two buildings back to the local people.

On the south side of the property at the Traverse City State Hospital was the Arnell Engstrom School. It was believed that school-age inmates at the state hospital needed to be separated from the adult patients, and Arnell, a well-liked state representative for the area, was instrumental in getting state money to build this school. He had an insurance agency in Traverse City, the Engstrom-Hicks Insurance Company, was in the legislature for a long time, and was chairman of the House appropriations committee for many years as well.

When the hospital was closed, there was a question of what to do with this particular building. At the same time, the Traverse Bay Intermediate School District, which had raised one million dollars to build a new building, realized the Arnell Engstrom building was suitable for what they needed and was actually a much better structure. After all, it was built like a fortress with brick walls and steel.

It seemed incomprehensible that the Intermediate School District would go out and build a new building when this one was available. Why not have them pay the state one million dollars and buy this building? I talked to Governor John Engler about it and eventually that is what happened.

About the same time, the Northern Michigan Children's Clinic, which had been working out of Munson Medical Center for many, many years, was looking for office space. Here again was another organization that served children. Bill Brady was operating it at the time, and Lieutenant Governor Connie Binsfeld was very close to that particular program. When the deal was made to transfer the Arnell Engstrom School to the Intermediate School District, the Northern Michigan Children's Clinic was given a portion of the building space with which carry out its activities. This was accomplished over opposition from some members of Governor Engler's budget committee and others, but eventually we got the job done.

The rest of the state hospital property was handled through a redevelopment corporation under a special act the legislature passed in the 1940s to allow local units of government to set up quasi-private development corporations on these kinds of properties. In this particular case, it's even more interesting because the state hospital property is split—part of it is in Garfield Township and part of it is in Traverse City. In fact, there's some question about where the line actually is, because the hospital is so old the lines were never distinctly drawn. Some of the buildings even appear to straddle the line! In order to accommodate both units of government, a law was needed, so I introduced one that would allow townships to operate in concurrence with cities so that the two units of government together could form a redevelopment corporation to accept the property from the state and develop it, which ultimately came about.

A lot of the state hospital property had been previously sold off, but roughly 450 acres remained surrounding the main campus on the west side of Traverse City. The Garfield Township people were interested in having a big portion of what was in the township (one hundred acres) preserved as a park. This area included a wooded area and a hill that produced artesian wells that really couldn't or shouldn't be built on anyway.

On the east side of the property, along Kids Creek, were wetlands unsuitable for other uses. The city wanted those particular properties preserved as a park, so a big chunk of the property was transferred to Garfield Township and the City of Traverse City for park purposes.

The center core of the campus was transferred to the redevelopment corporation for one dollar, with the understanding that the northern part of it, next to Munson Medical Center and the county medical care facility, would eventually be sold to those two entities for roughly two million dollars and that money would be used to develop the rest of the campus. Unfortunately, other activities got involved that have not been completely settled at this time. However, that was the original intention, and through this means the state was able to transfer the entire 510 acres for one dollar. The idea was that the balance of the property had a negative value, and when coupled with the positive value on the area that Munson and the Med Care wanted, would bring the equation to one. Had the state sold the property to those units directly, the money would have gone to the state and the two organizations would have been left with the undeveloped property.

Four other parcels in the real estate transaction are to be sold to the Grand Traverse Redevelopment Corporation, or the Commons board as it is now called. As of this time, that sale hasn't taken place that I am aware of. The whole idea is to transfer this property to local units of government on a fair market basis with the exception of those parts that are to be preserved as parks for public use.

The site also had two hundred feet of bay frontage in Bingham Township in Leelanau County. This land was donated to the state hospital many years earlier as a place where the inmates and patients could swim. It's a nice chunk of property at the end of Bingham Road on West Bay, and through the efforts of Senator John Pridnia, the senator for that particular county in 1990 when we were working on this transaction, the bay frontage and park land on West Bay were donated to Bingham Township, again for one dollar. I had the pleasure of making the presentation of that deed in 1994 to the Bingham Township Board as John had retired.

When I went into the legislature in 1990, all these property transactions were in the works. I was not only involved in the Arnell Engstrom facility transaction and the balance of the state hospital property, I also represented the State Regional Psychiatric Hospital in Newberry, Michigan, in Luce County up in the U.P. A sizeable unit was closed there as well, and the disposition needed to be worked out between the village of Newberry and a couple of surrounding townships that were connected in terms of water and sewer. That problem has only partially been resolved. The opportunities for utilizing those buildings are not as great as they are in Traverse City, but the State Corrections Department, needing additional space, has taken over the west end of the property for a prison that will provide jobs in Luce County and be a good use of those buildings. The use of the east end of the campus still is undecided.

Anytime there is a major change like this, pros and cons surface and discussions become heated. The decision to close the Traverse City State Hospital was made before I was in the legislature. Arnell Engstrom School closed the first year I was in the legislature, and Newberry closed about the same time. Those changes were in the works before I arrived in Lansing, but a major part of my first four-year term dealt with those particular properties because they were both in my senatorial district.

I have mixed feelings about the preservation of the buildings on the former state hospital grounds. I think the idea of preserving the parklands is especially good. The Garfield Township part is wooded, but it does have a lot of springs, so the best use of that property is likely park land. It adds a nice dimension to Traverse City and Garfield Township.

The buildings themselves, outside of the chapel, which is very significant from my standpoint and also the Arnell Engstrom School, are very significant. They are well built and fairly modern. There is some question about the other buildings. I think some are going on the historical preservation list. Others are being restored and used under the leadership of Ray Minervini, a monumental effort.

Probably the most significant thing about many of the oldest buildings is that they were built with Markham brick, a brick made in the Greilickville area. It's a local brick, light in color; a special railroad was built from Greilickville to the state hospital to transport those bricks for the construction of the older buildings, particularly Building 50. Of course, there are thousands and thousands and thousands of Markham bricks. Markham was a cherry grower in the early days, but he also made his money in the brick yard.

My house on Garfield Road is made from the same kind of brick, but these particular bricks were made in Beitner rather than Greilickville. It's not a hard brick; it's soft compared to some others, and its longevity has yet to be seen. Some of it has been there pretty near one hundred years.

Though the buildings do not have the same significance for me that they do for many of the new people who have moved into our area more recently, the campus is very beautiful with lots of trees and grass, so it is a valuable addition to the City of Traverse City and also to Garfield Township and is developing nicely.

Chapter Four

Local Geography and Related Stories

Peninsula Township is one of the most interesting townships in the state of Michigan from many, many standpoints. Geographically, the tip on the north end of the peninsula rests on the 45th parallel, which is halfway between the equator and the North Pole. If you follow that line around the earth, you'll find some interesting places that are quite different in climate from the Old Mission Peninsula. In spite of how far north it is, thanks to being surrounded by water on three sides, the peninsula has a maritime climate.

Governmentally speaking, the peninsula is the equivalent of three towns long and two towns wide and includes the island now known as Power Island that in my day was called Ford's Island and before that Marion Island. All told, the peninsula contains pieces of four different townships. The first settlement, Old Mission, was on the north end of the peninsula. The peninsula also was the first township designated in Grand Traverse County.

Today people talk about being from Traverse City and approach the peninsula from south to north, but the original settlers approached from north to south. Think about it: in those days, travel was by boat. The original settlers came down the Great Lakes from St. Ignace and Mackinaw City to the "great crossing" between Charlevoix and Leelanau counties. The settlement we now know as Old Mission was called Grand Traverse, or in French, "Le Grande Traverse." The native Americans called it "The Great Crossing" because if they wanted to go down the coastline of Lake Michigan in their canoes, they had to swing from Atwood across the water to the tip of the Leelanau Peninsula and down across that vast area.

The first post office in Grand Traverse County was called the Post Office of Grand Traverse and was at the village of present Old Mission. That post office is older than the post office in Traverse City. In fact, it's kind of interesting how the Traverse City post office got its name. In the early 1850s, Tracy Lay, one of the Hannah and Lay founders of Traverse City, traveled to Washington, D.C. to get a post office for the new community. He proposed to the clerk in Washington that the new post office be called the Post Office of Grand Traverse City. The clerk said it would be too confusing to have the Post Office of Grand Traverse (out at Old Mission on the peninsula) and the Post Office of Grand Traverse City. He suggested that Lay drop the "Grand," and that's how the Traverse City Post Office got its name.

The Post Office of Grand Traverse handled the mail from the Straights of Mackinac to Manistee by boat in the summer and in the winter by sled over the ice. The name "Grand Traverse" was changed to "Old Mission" after the Indians moved out of that settlement to Omena in Leelanau County in the Peshawbetown area where they live today. "Omena" apparently means "New Mission," so "Grand Traverse" was eventually changed to "Old Mission" after the Indians made the move.

Three towers were built on the peninsula over the years. The Frederich Tower, which used to be located at the top of Carroll Hill on the east side of the road across from the Chateau Grand Traverse, was one of the first tourist activities in the region. Built by businessmen in Traverse City in about 1923, it was a beautiful place. You could climb the three-story tower and view the whole countryside, including both bays, from the highest point on the peninsula. Great-grandfather Peter Carroll's youngest son, Charlie Carroll, lived with his family in the house on the property just to the east of the tower. At one time they had a store in the tower with knickknacks to tempt the tourists. When I was a lad, a three-inch pipe went from the first floor to the top floor with a sign that said, "If the view pleases you, please drop coins here." Many tourists made voluntary donations to keep up the tower until it finally became so unsafe it had to be torn down.

The Golden Tower was on Eiman Road, off one end of the Golden farm that was eventually owned by Oliver Tompkins, his mother having been a Golden. A third tower was built just across the road from the Frederich Tower after the end of World War II as part of the civil defense system of the United States. Four heavy telephone poles were put in the ground and a platform was built toward the top with a little shack. Along with everyone else in the neighborhood, I spent time there on a voluntary basis observing planes that might be flying under the radar. Of course, we were told the Sault Locks were one of the most important defense spots in the nation. Eventually, someone decided we didn't need to watch for low-flying planes anymore and the tower was torn down.

Grand Traverse Bay, a very unique body of water worldwide, is a major part of the environment of the northwestern part of the Lower Peninsula. It funnels down toward Traverse City into two arms, the east and west arms of Grand Traverse Bay, or East Bay and West Bay. Grand Traverse Bay itself extends clear from Northport across to Atwood and plays a huge role in the history of the region. In the first place, in terms of the climate, it's always interesting that the longest growing season in the county, or the area with the most days above freezing, is at its northernmost point, on the tip of the Old Mission Peninsula. There it's possible to have as many as 150 growing days a year because of the warming influence of the water. Contrast that with the shortest growing season in Grand Traverse County, or the place with the fewest days above freezing, which is in the southernmost point at Fife Lake. The number of frost-free days there can be as few as seventy-five. Many times it's even warmer in the winter on the peninsula than in Lansing or Detroit, provided the bays have open water. In the summer, of course, there's the opposite effect, and the bays have a somewhat cooling influence on the area.

Along with the water, the prevailing winds in the winter and spring are usually out of the northwest, so the wind has to come over the water before it hits the land. It comes over Lake Michigan first and then over West Bay and then across. The wind carrying those warm air currents from the water provides a good horticultural base.

All this was recognized in the middle 1800s by early horticulturalists. H. M. Cleveland, writing for the *Atlantic Monthly*, projected that the western side of the land mass of the state of Michigan would be especially suitable for the growth of horticultural crops. Sure enough, many of the early settlers on the peninsula grew different types of fruit. Not cherries so much to start with, but peaches and apples and then eventually cherries.

In the early days, the bays provided a vital transportation link for the agricultural industry and Bowers Harbor provided the refuge for sailing vessels that carried potatoes and apples and other crops up and down the lakes. The same was true for Old Mission Harbor, the other harbor on the peninsula. The Haserot Cherry Factory at Northport had a substation at Old Mission, and cherries were transported across the bay from Old Mission to Northport. There was also some shipping of apples and potatoes by boat to Chicago and other ports in the early days.

The bays also provided a link for the timber industry. Land was cleared for farming and logs were sold and quite often had to be transported to Traverse City. If the bays froze smoothly, they made an excellent highway for horses and sleighs carrying logs, though it could be a little dangerous sometimes. My grandfather talked about going uphill all the way to Traverse City on the ice, meaning that in the spring of the year the ice could become quite pliable, so if you had a heavy weight of logs, sometimes the back runners would drop a little lower than the front ones. It made you keep moving up the bay all right, but it was still much more convenient than going over land.

Farmers and landowners also used to stack cord wood along the bay to be picked up by sailing vessels. At the head of East Bay, at Mitchell Creek, and no doubt on West Bay at the Boardman River Sawmills, wood was sawed and floated out in the bay and loaded onto schooners to be taken up and down the lakes.

Before we had electric refrigerators, we had ice boxes. On West Bay, at the mouth of the Boardman River, there used to be an icehouse. In the winter, the ice was marked and cut out of the bay with a saw that looked something like a cross cut saw and then packed in sawdust. Every Saturday, we would stop in town and pick up a block of ice and bring it home to put in the ice box before the days of electric refrigerators.

The bays also provided an abundant source of food for the area. My grandfather talked about sturgeon being a major fish in the bay. People would fish the sturgeon and stack them up like cords of wood on the shores, either at Willow Point, a deep inlet on East Bay, or other spots, and sailing vessels would come in and pick up the sturgeon and take them away.

Whitefish, cisco, and trout were also important fish. At the south end of East Bay, on what we now call the Miracle Mile, much of the area was owned by a man named Otto West who had a fishing pier. When I was a young lad back in the '30s, we used to stop at West Fishery and pick up cisco or whitefish or trout to have as a meal.

Succors were also an important fish from the bay. Smoked succors are very good, as well as fried, boiled, broiled, canned, pickled, or any other way you'd care to fix them. Few people eat them today, but we ate a lot of them in the '30s and the '40s and we weren't the only ones. In fact, succor spearing was always one of the interesting things we did in the spring. They're very good out of the bay with its good, clean, clear water. One problem, of course, is the "Y" bones in the tail. If they're pickled in vinegar, the bones dissolve and they're actually quite good, but if Ma fried or boiled them (she usually fried them), you had to be very careful of the bones, but they were good eating anyway. Grandma McManus used to boil them. Her kitchen was the first place I ever saw fish and potatoes boiled in the same pot, but she used to do that regularly. Succor was a good fish and provided a lot of sustenance for Peninsula Township residents.

At one point in time, carp were also in plentiful supply in the bay. In the spring of the year, you could watch schools of carp with their backs sticking out of the water going up the bay. We never ate carp, though they were commercially harvested and sold to the New York market. There was a lot of talk about it, but we never ate them at our place. I always heard that the way to cook a carp was to gut it out, clean it, nail it to a board, and put it in the oven and bake it for several hours. When it was done, throw the carp away and eat the board! People kind of shied away from it. Apparently it had an odor, unless it was properly handled.

Smelt were quite plentiful at one time, too. We didn't harvest them on the peninsula, but I went smelt dipping in creeks in Leelanau County where they came in great numbers. In recent days, coho salmon have been planted and there's been some reintroduction of trout and whitefish after their demise from the lamprey eel, which took out a good chunk of the fishing industry at the time. Fishing through the ice remains quite common as well.

At one time there was a dance hall on Bassett Island, a little island just to the north of Power Island toward Neahtawanta Point, and a boat made an excursion from Traverse City out to the dance hall and back several nights a week. More recently, there's a lot of yachting and other types of recreational activity on the bay, but local traffic on the lakes was a lot more prevalent one hundred years ago than it is today. My own grandfather McManus sailed the lakes in his early days and he told me about a major trip he made that convinced him to get out of the business.

He'd gotten on a sailing vessel at Bowers Harbor with a load of cordwood to go to St. Ignace. It always seemed kind of odd to me to haul cordwood from the peninsula to St. Ignace because they appear to have plenty of wood in the St. Ignace area, but for whatever reason they loaded up and set sail and then a storm came up. This wasn't unusual for Lake Michigan, but it was nighttime and the storm got bad and eventually they threw the wood overboard to lighten the vessel. Finally all the crew went down in the hold to await the inevitable, but Grandpa said he stayed up at the tiller all night and rode out the storm there. He always said that when they went around Wagashance Point in Emmet County at the north end of the lake, he could feel the ship scrape bottom. They finally made it into the straights and the storm subsided, but all he had on was a pea coat. His hands were frozen to the tiller (I suppose they locked up on him is what really happened) and the crew had to pry him loose. He said he'd never felt so cold in his life and it took him about three days to get warmed up. I don't know if that's what changed Grandpa from a sailor into a farmer, but it probably did convince him to move in some other direction.

By the way, Grandpa never learned to drive a car because he always claimed he tried to steer the automobile like you steered a tiller on a boat, in which case if you wanted to go left, you turned it to the right, and if you wanted to go right, you turned it to the left. He decided not to drive rather than change the way he steered.

Grandma never drove a car either after the experience she had one time when she was learning. She was supposed to hit the brake pedal but actually she hit the gas. She was out across the field before they got her stopped and she decided that was enough of that. Someone else could do the driving!

The bay is also a source of drinking water for Traverse City. In the early days the water was piped from West Bay, but it was decided later on—probably for good reason, since the city sewer dumped into the Boardman River which in turn dumped into West Bay—that maybe the water should come from East Bay.

The bay has had its share of tragedies. Both bays are quite deep in spots, the deepest point on East Bay being just off Old Mission. There's a spot off Ford Island in West Bay that's also very deep, and with depth goes cold water. One of the old tales about the bays is that they never give up their dead. In such cold water, drowning victims stay down.

One incident I remember from my youth concerned a skating accident in Bowers Harbor. If the bay froze on a still night, the skating was just great, but you had to be careful not to venture out to the softer, mushier spots. Skating also became dangerous in the spring, when the ice was beginning to thaw. I remember this particular accident because I was quite young and they were talking about how to find the body. Some people said that if you put mercury in a loaf of bread and set it adrift on the bay, it would supposedly come to rest over the body.

Another tragedy involved a well-known local industrialist named Pete Rennie. He had been out on his iceboat on West Bay and just disappeared and no one ever determined what happened to him. One theory is that a soft spot exists in the ice in an area just south of Power Island where there's an underground spring that pushes up warm water, preventing the ice from freezing as thick as it does in other parts of the bay. Thus, it was always speculated he went down in that area. Other people who've done a lot of fishing have told me the Native Americans also recognized that particular spot in the bay.

Most everyone is acquainted with the two harbors on the peninsula, Bowers Harbor and Old Mission, but there's a third deep spot along East Bay at Robinsons' Point that not many people think about. My grandmother told me that in the very old days, sailing vessels used to land there to pick up cordwood. I know it's a deep harbor because when I was a young lad, when we'd go succor spearing with Ed Bopry. At Robinson's Point if you had been wading, you had to go right up on land because the deep water came so close to the shore. That area's all residential now, and probably nobody ever thinks about landing a sailing vessel there anymore. It was called Willow Point in my day and may have been the harbor originally for the village of Archie.

No matter where I travel in the world, I never cease to be amazed at the beauty and grandeur of the east and west arms of Grand Traverse Bay. We took the water for granted when we were growing up; we saw both bays every day and accepted them as part of life. But as you travel around the world and see other places, hardly anything compares with the sights of Grand Traverse Bay.

Medicinally, things were a little different in those days. My mother kept a hot water bottle in the closet along with a tube that had an injector on the end of it. Her common cure for most everything from the cold on down was an enema. If we came up with some reason why we didn't want to go to school, mother would usually head for the closet and get that enema bottle. We suddenly decided we felt better and were off, because nobody was particularly interested in one of those experiences. In those days, they filled that hot water bottle about half full with lukewarm water and added soap so they had a kind of soapy medium. Then they turned you backside up and you got an enema. That cured whatever ailed you, usually.

If you had a bad cold, mother would also put a mustard plaster on your chest or something that was the equivalent of Vicks Vapor Rub and the fumes and the grease usually cured you in a couple of days. I'm not sure but what we'd have gotten cured just as quick without it, but that was the standard practice.

Toothaches and earaches plagued us. We had ointments for earaches, but the liniments weren't all that effective. Also, dental hygiene was very poor in those days. Everyone seemed to understand cleanliness and germs and standard health practices of most kinds, but they weren't up to speed on dental. We were never required to brush our teeth and our parents didn't either. My father had false teeth as long as I can remember. My mother didn't. She had a pretty good set of teeth, but eventually they gave her toothaches.

The medicine we used usually came from the Raleigh man. Every community had a roving peddler called a Raleigh man. Adolph Viskochil was ours, and he came regularly with his little suitcases of various things. He had lots of women's fingernail polish and hair lotions and perfumes that he attempted to sell, as well as certain kinds of food products. Pepper was the main one. Pert' near all the women in our area had a big box of Raleigh's Pepper on the back of the stove.

He also sold Raleigh's Anti-Pain Oil, which was primarily methyl alcohol. You used that if you had any kind of a sore or toothache or earache or whatever else. He had Bag Baum for the cows, too, so he was kind of the medicine man for a lot of common, ordinary ailments.

Talking about Raleigh's Anti-Pain Oil, I remember my cousin John Gallagher and I were out to a party one night. It must have been in the middle '40s. I don't know if we were in high school yet, but rather than go home, since we were late, we decided to go to Grandma McManus' house. She always had what they called a "new part" on the east end of the house. The house had been built with two bedrooms upstairs and an addition with an extra room that was never finished. It was always called "the new part." It had been the new part, I suppose, for forty years. But there were some extra beds there, and whenever we'd go to Grandma's, if we came down in the morning and weren't feeling all that well, she would reach up in the cupboard and get that bottle of Raleigh's Anti-Pain Oil and mix a tablespoon in a half glass of water for each of us. She'd say, "This is always what I gave my boys when they were feelin' a little off in the morning." She had seven of them, so I guess she knew what she was doing. I looked at that bottle of Raleigh's Anti-Pain Oil one day and in plain English in large letters it said, "*For External Use Only.*"

In the spring every year, one of the first items my mother would get from the yard was dandelion greens. My wife still does that. Ma would go out and dig up the emerging dandelions just as they began to grow and make wilted dandelion greens with vinegar and onion. She always called that her spring tonic. Some people used sulphur and molasses, but we never had to. Of course, we were off to the woods as soon as the mushrooms came along and we collected as many morels as we could. That was a very good treat in the spring of the year.

As soon as cherries were harvested, we'd usually go out to Grandpa Fromholz' place and he'd take us into what we called the Pine Plains to go huckleberryin'. This was the area around Arbutus and Spider lakes up east of the area where I live now. Nowadays people call them blueberries, but we went in the woods and picked huckleberries. Quite an extended period of time would yield half a pail full, but they were excellent. You'd bring those back and clean them up and then mother and grandmother—you usually divided them—would make pies, and there's nothing like huckleberry pie made from real huckleberries. They have a little stronger flavor than cultivated blueberries. Grandpa used to say, "H-you-huckle: B-you-buckle: Y-huckleberry pie." He really liked his huckleberry pie.

In the fall of the year, we'd gather blackberries from the woods at home. We'd get almost enough off our own place wild, but we also sometimes went blackberrying in other parts of the county up on state land. If there was an excess beyond what we ate within a few days of the pickings, mother would can them and we'd have canned blackberries (or canned blueberries) in the wintertime, which could be eaten as a sauce or made into a pie.

Mother did a lot of canning. She canned light sweet cherries and dark sweet cherries but also sour cherries with sugar. We ate canned sour cherries for dessert many, many times a year. Very few people do that nowadays. The industry doesn't can the sour cherries in sugar; they're canned in water so they can be used as a diabetic pack. Canned in sugar, they have an excellent flavor and they're a fine item for dessert after meals.

It's kind of interesting that in the '30s and '40s on the peninsula when I was growing up, alcohol was pretty much taboo. There weren't any bars and no one suggested there should be, but if you go back into the initial records of Peninsula Township, you find that things were a little different. The first order of business at Carlos and Campbell's store in Old Mission was to organize the township of Peninsula, but the second order of business was to acquire a liquor license for the sale of alcoholic spirits for mechanical and medicinal purposes! Apparently, in the very early days, alcohol wasn't quite as taboo as it was when I was raised, which followed prohibition. Now you go up the peninsula and there's two or three bars and several wineries and nobody thinks anything of it, but drinking alcohol was a pretty big subject in my young days.

About 1964, which would be thirty or so years later, my dad decided to sell the home farm, that same forty-five acres he'd bought in 1935, and he told me to go over to the Charlie Lyons family to the south of us, neighbors of ours for many, many years, and offer it to them for $55,000 cash. My father wanted to move out to Garfield Road because the rest of the family had farms there. We hadn't been able to buy land on the peninsula because it wasn't for sale, and he wanted to be out amongst his kids.

I didn't find out how he'd initially managed to acquire the land until he sent me over to the Lyons. At Lyons, we were sitting around talking about the land and finally we got around to the price. I said, "Dad told me to tell you he'd sell that farm for $55,000 cash."

Charlie said, "Give me a few minutes to talk to the boys out in the kitchen."

He and his sons Bob and Bruce went out to the kitchen while I sat in the living room with Bertha and Beverly. Bertha was Mrs. Lyons, and Beverly was their daughter. She worked at the city for many, many years.

Finally the men came back into the living room and wanted to know if we'd throw in a floating drag that was sittin' up by the woods. We always had a floating drag we used in the orchard that we stored up by the woods. The Lyonses needed a floatin' drag, so acting on my own, I said we'd throw it in and the deal was made.

I went back home. My dad was sitting in the living room in his big chair. I told him we had a deal with the Lyonses if I'd throw in the floatin' drag and I'd said we would. He said, "Oh yah, that's okay. It's good enough." Then he added, "I figured they'd take the deal!"

I said, "How in the world did you figure that?"

"Well," he said, "the last time they had a chance to buy this farm was in 1935 from your Uncle Alfie. At that time Uncle Alfie told them he wanted $2,500 for the place and Charlie tried to get the price down. He offered him $2,000. Now you had to know your Uncle Alfie. He and his Irish brogue says, 'And sure if they wanted it for $25,000 they wouldn't get it!"

Uncle Alfie made a rather solid decision not to sell it to the Lyonses in 1935 but to offer it to somebody else. My dad, his nephew, was the somebody else. Uncle Alfie made a deal with my dad on a land contract deal for the forty-five acres and the house and barn for $4,000 at four percent interest, payable at the rate of one hundred dollars a year on the principle, plus the interest. Furthermore, if they would keep Uncle Alfie and provide room and board, they didn't have to pay the interest and would only have to pay one hundred dollars a year on the principal.

We started out with that arrangement, but it didn't last too long. Uncle Alfie was a confirmed bachelor and a very independent old codger. He wore a big gray overcoat and went into town on Saturdays like most farmers to buy groceries and play cards (usually at the Board of Trade), and he'd bring home a sack of orange candy and give my brother and me one piece a day.

Well, we got smart one time and decided we were going to find out where that candy was. He had the north bedroom upstairs and we had the south bedroom. We got into his room when he wasn't home and found the overcoat and sack of candy and we proceeded to eat the whole thing. As you can imagine, that was the last time we ever got any orange candy from Uncle Alfie!

But that wasn't what caused him to end up not living with us. Uncle Alfie had lived with his mother for many years until she died and then had lived by himself. The fact is, he was fussy about what he ate. Mainly he didn't eat much variety. He liked boiled Irish potatoes and fried salt pork. In those days when they butchered hogs, they cut the pork into squares and put the squares in a barrel of heavy salt water for preservation. When they were ready to cook it, they'd bring it out and freshen it by soaking it in fresh water to get some of the salt out and then slice and fry it with the rind on. The pork was mostly fat, but they'd fry it until it was crisp, saving the hot grease. Then they'd boil potatoes, put the boiled potatoes on the plate, mash them with a fork, pour the hot pork grease over the top with a little salt and pepper, and eat the potatoes with the fried side pork. Fixing this was the best thing you could do for Uncle Alfie. It's what he wanted, and he'd just as soon eat it seven days a week.

The problem was, my mother was German and she loved to cook. She was a good cook and made a variety of things, all of which my dad enjoyed, but not Uncle Alfie. He got to complainin' and my dad put up with it for a while, but one morning Uncle Alfie went down to the barn and started up again about that German woman my dad was married to and her cooking. My dad finally put a stop to it and told him he guessed it was time he moved out.

For a while Uncle Alfie moved in with Aunt Janie Buchan and Uncle Will on the west shore, and when his money ran out, he moved in with Aunt Addie Coolidge, my grandfather's sister, on Island View Road and M-37. Uncle Alfie lived to be eighty-nine years old, fat salt pork or no fat salt pork!

Chapter Five

Agriculture and . . . Yep, Related Stories

Grandpa McManus mostly farmed with horses, but towards the end of his life Uncle Carl got a tractor, a McCormick-Deering, and he taught Grandpa how to drive it. It didn't have a starter; it was the kind you started with a crank. Grandpa would get her goin' and disk or drag or whatever, but eventually the tractor got so it was difficult, if not impossible, to shift from neutral into gear if the engine was running. Grandpa couldn't get it shifted, so he'd bring it up to the house, which sat on the top of a hill, turn it around and head it back downhill so it had a pretty good grade, and then shut her off with the drag behind it. When he wanted to go to work, he'd get around in front of the tractor and turn the crank. Since it was heading downhill, he could turn the engine over and the tractor would start. Then he'd run around behind and slip in between the drag and the tractor and jump up on the seat. It didn't exactly follow all the safety rules and regulations, but it got the job done until Uncle Carl caught him at it and made him quit.

I remember my Uncle Carl; he was a very patient man. At my grandfather's farm, they were down to one cow they milked for family use, but of course she needed to be bred once a year. The nearest bull was at one of the neighbors, about a mile down the road. I was just a young lad at the time, but I remember going to the barn with Uncle Carl, who told me the cow was in heat and needed to be taken to the bull. He put a chain around her neck and started to lead her on the road toward the neighbors.

He hadn't gotten too far when the cow decided she wanted to go back to the barn, and in the process of changing her mind, she took him down over a thorny side hill. Of course Uncle Carl got a few scrapes, not only to his body, but to his personality. In a very calm, cool manner, he harnessed up the horses and hooked them to the wagon and then hooked Bossy by her chain to the wagon. He got in the wagon and said, "Gid up."

The horses started up the hill and got about as far as before when old Bossy again decided she wasn't going any further. I remember my uncle very calmly sitting on the seat, saying to the horses, "Gid up." When Bossy hit the end of that chain, it was either a case of moving forward or having her neck pulled off. After she dragged the first hundred feet or so, she didn't have any trouble at all walking up the road. They went the mile and got her bred and brought her home and life went on.

Granddad never had much money. He was quite poor all his life, but in later years my Aunt Dorothy worked in town. She lived with Grandpa and Grandma and took care of them. She spent money to buy groceries and take care of the other expenses around the house. Grandpa and Grandma were getting small checks (I suppose either supplemental or Social Security or something) and Grandma would contribute hers to the buying of groceries, but Grandpa wasn't comin' forth. They knew he was tucking away a little money under the linoleum up in his bedroom—he slept in his own bedroom by that time—so one day they asked him if he'd like to contribute a little money to buying the groceries. Grandpa said, "Why sure; how much is a sack of flour?" He was willing to put up enough to buy a twenty-five-pound sack of flour once in a while!

When you think about it, those people didn't spend a lot of money for anything except making sure they had their taxes paid. They raised potatoes, had a cow for their milk, and Grandma usually kept some chickens for the eggs. They'd get fish from the bay and sometimes butcher a hog and once in a great while they had beef, but that was pretty unusual. They had a garden, and Grandma canned vegetables and fruit, so their necessities from town weren't all that great. She got by all her life without very much from the grocery store other than salt, sugar, and flour, and she could cook up a meal out of not very much as long as she had salt pork and potatoes and a few other basics.

Dad always said, for breakfast, they had cornmeal six days a week and oatmeal on Sundays! She raised eleven children and lived to the ripe old age of eighty-seven on not very much of anything. Granddad was always neat and well dressed when he was in public, worked hard all his life, and for his part lived into his nineties.

Grandma Fromholz was quite an outstanding lady. In 1935, elected by farmers from the neighborhood, she became master of the East Bay Grange. Back then, the Grange was *the* farm organization in Michigan, and I expect those masters generally were men. Some Granges still exist today and have a voice in agriculture, but back then they were very important. They preceded Farm Bureau and were an important source of agricultural information as well as a community gathering place.

My grandparents Arthur Thomas and wife Eliza Jane (Carroll) McManus

There were several grange halls in Michigan; one of them was at the intersection of Rusch and Garfield Roads, on land I now own, across the road from my house. My grandparents were founders of that grange and participated for many, many years. My mother became a member in the '20s and my parents danced there. The halls were built so they could have official meetings, somewhat like a lodge, but there was also a stage where performances could be held, with the floors typically hardwood so people could dance. Eventually, in the East Bay Grange, another room was added for a kitchen so they could put on dinners, social events, and potlucks. This was the gathering place for the neighborhood, and the master was elected by the rest of the members and was in charge of activities for that particular year.

My dad always told me it was kind of a touchy affair when he started courting my mother and showed up at the East Bay Grange hall for the weekly dance one Saturday night. Apparently my grandparents (or at least my grandmother) had another fellow in mind for my mother and they weren't too sure about this Irishman from the peninsula coming out to dance with their daughter. Some of her cousins weren't all that excited about it either, but eventually Dad was accepted by the group and got to be a pretty good friend of Bill Strohm and some of my mother's other cousins in the Blair and East Bay Township .

At the time Clara and I were courting in the 1940s, her parents were active members in a Grange headquartered in Grawn. Parents with teenage children had instituted Saturday night dances, and the hall still stands where those dances were conducted. We danced on the second floor and they had a kitchen on the first floor where they made hamburgers and hotdogs at midnight. At least three generations of people typically danced—the grandparents, the parents, and the teenagers. The music included square dances as well as the fox trot, the two-step,rye waltzes and so on, courtesy of a three-piece orchestra out of Manton that consisted of a piano player, a drummer, and a saxophone. Most of the young folks west and south of Traverse City went to Grawn for the grange dances on Saturday nights. It was a good, clean activity for young people, and the parents took an active part not only in sponsoring it but being part of the activity.

There were other dances on the weekends, too. I remember going with my cousin, John Gallagher, to Summit City one night to the

Grange dance over there. My cousin, Vesper McManus from Kingsley, attended those dances as well.

There was even a Cherryland Grange on the peninsula whose meetings were held in the town hall since they didn't have a separate grange hall. They put on dances too, but I think I only attended one of those. My attentions were drawn to the Grawn area from the time I was old enough to dance until I eventually got married.

There were also commercial dance halls in the Traverse City area. One of the biggest was at Rusch's on Rusch Road just a mile west of where we now live. Frank Rusch and his wife Stella and their boys conducted dances there, with Stella playing the piano and the boys playing various musical instruments. That was a very popular place, and though I never attended a dance there, my wife Clara did, along with her brother Dick.

Earlier, a dance hall operated at Oatka Beach on Four Mile Road at the U.S. 31 intersection. Now a condominium sits there instead of a dance pavilion. I attended a couple of dances there and I've also heard my father talk about a dance hall in Traverse City called the Gardens that many people attended, probably back in the 1920s. Dance halls were places where people in the community, particularly young people, could come together, get to know one another, and do their courting.

Back in the fall of the year, when we first had the farm, we harvested a lot of old apple varieties. My great-uncle Alfred had planted an apple orchard, and in those days you planted several varieties so you could harvest and sell over a period of time. We had Alexanders and Wolf Rivers and Baldwins and Snow Apples and Spitzenburgs and Bellflowers and Jonathons and Wealthies and Wagoners and Opalescence—many, many different varieties. They didn't have a lot of commercial value except during World War II, but even so, the first money I ever made was picking up apples from the orchard and taking them into Morgan's Cider Mill in Traverse City and selling them for fifty dollars, which was a lot of money.

We also used to press our own cider. In order to make good cider, you need a variety of apples, and some of those old varieties were excellent. You take something like Talman Sweets, which is a very sweet apple, and mix it with a Baldwin, a very tart apple, and put the two together and maybe mix in two or three other varieties and you come up with an excellent apple cider. The cider nowadays is usually made from just a few varieties. It's an acceptable product, but it has nowhere near the flavor of the old cider made from six, eight, or ten varieties of apples.

Water from the bay was also used by many peninsula farmers for spraying their orchards. That was the big source of water before wells were as prevalent as they are today. Farmers who lived on or close to the bay often used a mechanism on their sprayers called an aspirator. If you showed up at the bay with an empty tank, you had to bail out a few pails of water by hand to prime the pump, and then with the engine running, the aspirator would suck the water—though that's not the proper term—and aspirate the suction hose so that atmospheric pressure would drive the bay water into the tank. In this way you could fill a three- or four- hundred-gallon tank in short order without having to dip the whole thing with a five-gallon pail.

The early machines were pulled by horses down to the bay. After the water from the bay filled the tank, the machine was driven back to the farm and pesticides were added.

I always heard the story that one of the farmers got a little too far out in the bay one day with his sprayer. The early sprayer tanks were all made of wood, and for some reason his wasn't fastened down very well. Once he got into deep water, the empty tank floated off the carriage and began drifting down the bay. He had to retrieve it and put his rig back together before he could proceed with the job!

My grandfather and dad operated a little differently. When it came time to spray, my grandfather would take the horse and a stone boat (all the farms had stone boats in those days, which consisted of a couple of posts hewed on one end so they would act as runners with 2 x 6's or 2 x 8's nailed across and then bolted so you could operate the boat as a float for hauling wood or potatoes or anything else rather than use a wheelbarrow or wagon). He'd put four fifty-gallon barrels on the stone boat and drive down to the bay. With a pail, he'd bail those four barrels of water full and put a washtub over the top of each one to try to hold the water. Then he'd drive the stone boat and those four barrels of water back to the farm, where he'd use a pail to bail the water out of those barrels into the spray tank. It's hard to imagine anybody going to that length today to get spray water, but that's the way it was done originally.

Looking for a better way as the orchard was getting bigger, my dad knew there was a wet spot in the woods on the side hill of the farm, and eventually we dug it out and created a spring. I was old enough to help, so I expect it was in the early 1940s. We got enough two-inch pipe to put from the bottom of that spring to the foot of the hill, which was probably a drop of twenty feet vertically, but we had to go a much greater distance to get down the hill. It was sufficient to put a six- or seven-foot riser at the bottom with a fill pipe for a sprayer with a shut-off valve. Then we just let the sprayer fill by gravity, which was a major improvement over the previous system. Dad planted our original trees in 1929, so the water-bailed-out-of-the-bay system must have worked for eight or ten years.when the trees were young.

Grandpa Edward Carroll, Dad always said, was the fruit grower of the family, but the fruit-growing part of our lives really came from Grandma McManus (Liza Jane, we called her) more than from my grandfather. Grandpa would have been better off, Dad said, if he'd been born in Indiana where he could had had lots of corn and raised hogs, because he always loved to raise hogs, which he kept mainly for his own use. The farm on the peninsula with the sandy ground wasn't really suitable for corn or hogs, and it was my grandmother who insisted he plant fruit, apples first and eventually cherries. Edward Carroll, her father, was a sizeable apple grower in the early days, planting fruit on the farms he had a mile north of the original homestead, which became the William Carroll farm.

Working with animals back when they were the main source of power was always a dangerous situation, and it's a wonder more people weren't killed. I can tell several stories of near misses, and one has to do with digging a well. Since this was before there was drilling equipment, wells had to be dug with a shovel. If you had to go fifty or seventy-five feet down, the hole had to be dug fairly wide at the top and some cribbing put in as you went down so it wouldn't cave in on the person digging it.

After you got down more than five or six feet, you also needed a system to take the dirt up to be dumped. This was usually accomplished with a tripod over the well with a pulley at the top. A rope with a bucket went down as far in the well as a man was digging, with something pulling on the other end of the rope. That was usually a horse, a patient older horse that didn't tend to be jumpy, because it was kind of dangerous to be down in the well and have anything happen to that tripod or bucket that would cause the bucket of dirt to fall back down on top of you when you were in the hole.

My dad said they were digging the well up at the Charley Carroll farm when he was a fairly young kid when he saw a near miss. Peter Carroll was my dad's great-grandfather; Charles Carroll was his half-cousin. He was watching a fellow with a horse pull a bucket of dirt up to the top of the hole and then take it out and dump it and run the bucket back down again. For some reason, the horse tended to stop about a foot or so before she should have, so the man continually had to move her another foot or two after she stopped. Well, he got impatient with that so he got a little stick, and when she got just about to stop, he hauled off and whacked her on the rear end. She didn't stop where she should have. Instead, she went a little too far and pulled the bucket up to the top of the tripod, at which point it came loose from the rope and fell back down the hole.

Luckily, the fellow at the bottom saw it coming and edged himself back into a corner so that it landed right in front of his feet. The next time the rope went up, he came with it and said he'd had enough diggin' for one day!

When I was growing up in that neighborhood, the orchards weren't as concentrated as they are today. Most of the farmers had a few cows and pigs and chickens, raised hay and corn and other crops, and had the orchard as a cash crop on the side. We had seven cows to milk, a team of horses, and kept some pigs. At one point we had chickens. Mother raised a garden, and there was an old apple orchard on our place originally and about five acres of cherries. My dad had set out thirteen acres of cherries on the land he inherited/bought from my granddad, but on the home farm we raised livestock and other crops as did every other farmer.

This was a vastly different agriculture than it is today or has been in recent years. Usually the farmers loaded up their produce on Saturdays, went to town, and sold their cream at Tach's Creamery or someplace else and their eggs and sometimes apples and other produce to Johnson's Grocery or some of the other stores in town for cash. Then the women shopped on Front Street while the men went to a place called the Board of Trade, next to Johnson's Grocery in the block between Cass and Park Streets on the south side of the street, to play cards and make conversation about farming and other activities.

Potatoes were a cash crop on the peninsula at one time, too. We never raised a lot of them, but when I was a boy, several farmers had five or ten acres of potatoes, and my grandfather was great on always "raising a patch of potatoes," as he said.

As very young lads, my brother and I had the job of picking up potatoes. Potatoes were dug by hand, and you got a penny a crate for picking up the small potatoes, while the big guys got a nickel a crate for picking up the big ones. I never could understand that, because it certainly takes a lot longer to pick up a crate of little potatoes than it does a crate of big ones. But of course the farmers didn't get any money for the little ones, which is probably why we only got a cent a crate for picking them up.

As I said earlier, the peninsula provides an ideal climate for fruit growing because of the northwesterly winds that come across Lake Michigan and eventually across the west arm of Grand Traverse Bay. The temperatures are warmer than they are inland during the winter, which delays the blossoming of the fruit trees a little bit in the spring so they're less apt to bloom in the frosty period. Also, the peninsula stays warm enough on frosty nights so the fruit doesn't freeze as easily, at least in the higher locations in the township.

From the beginning, the peninsula produced some fruit, mainly apples, but also some peaches and other crops. The cherry industry really didn't get going until the 1930s. The mechanical cherry pitter, which really made the industry, was invented in 1917, and it took a while for the trees to be planted on a commercial basis. Some large acreages were planted in the late 1920s, and by the 1950s and '60s, the peninsula was the center of the cherry business in the United States.

Dad made the decision about the end of World War II that he wanted to plant the whole farm to fruit. That was a major change and not looked upon very favorably by many of the neighbors. They were convinced you had to keep cows and have a steady income from the dairy and also raise hogs, chickens, and the garden for your own use. You certainly couldn't put all your eggs in one basket and rely on the fruit industry to provide a living!

Dad felt that if that was where the money was, why go at it half-heartedly? Why not plant the whole farm to fruit and get rid of the cows and the rest of the animals? That's what we did, and eventually the rest of the farmers did the same thing.

The first commercial canning on the peninsula was done by the Burkhardt family factory, located just to the south side of Carroll Hill. Though many kinds of fruit were processed there, most of the crops during my upbringing were hauled off the peninsula, either into Traverse City or shipped by boat to the Haserot Canning Factory over at Northport.

Coming out of the Great Depression and wondering how to obtain some measure of success and security in life, I decided early on I wanted to play both sides of the aisle in terms of public service and private business. Frankly, I didn't trust either system to provide what I thought I might need as I approached retirement. From the private standpoint, going into business—particularly the farming business, which I was brought up in and was interested in—had a lot of problems: cheap prices, low returns, frost, and so on. In many cases it was just plain difficult if not impossible to make any money. On the other hand, even though public service jobs provided steady employment at a wage, they were subject to the whims of politicians and others and might not last either.

In order to do a little bit of both, as I began to approach high school graduation, I made plans to go to college and become a mathematics teacher. I loved math and I thought I could do a good job of teaching it, so I entered Michigan State College with that as a major.

In the meantime, my dad had always promised each of us boys that if we stayed home and worked on the farm through grade school and high school at no wages, he would set us up in farming. Well, his idea of setting us up was a little different than ours. We thought that if we stayed home and worked for nothing until we were out of high school, he would buy us a farm, set us up, and finance it, but he insisted on a payback– fair enough, I suppose. He always said the only thing in life anybody was entitled to was an opportunity. He certainly didn't believe in entitlements and all kinds of rights that people talk about today. He felt, and I think he was probably right, that if you had an opportunity, what you made of the opportunity was up to you.

He added one more thing that I think was very important, and that is the importance of *always maintaining your reputation*. That meant be honest, pay your bills and pay them on time, don't steal, don't lie, and so on. We were brought up with the belief that you didn't tarnish your reputation, and you also didn't tarnish the reputation of the family. That was very good advice that I passed on to my own children.

I attended Michigan State over the objection of my parents, my dad in particular, who thought I ought to stay home and farm. Finally he acknowledged that while he didn't know what anybody was going to do with a college education, probably it wouldn't hurt if I paid attention to the right kinds of things while I was there. To his amazement, he learned there was an agricultural college at Michigan State that taught horticulture and so on. Consequently, he spent a good deal of my first Christmas vacation convincing me to switch from a math major to taking horticulture and coming back to farm.

I agreed to that, but times were very tough. I earned fifty cents an hour on the farm in the summertime. That and the scholarship I received put me through college, and I got married at the beginning of my sophomore year. I attended all three quarters of my freshman and sophomore years at Michigan State, but in order to make extra money, I stayed out of school the fall of my junior year and only attended college winter and spring. I worked that next summer and then in my senior year went fall and winter so I could finish up by the first of March. I actually completed my bachelors degree in ten quarters rather than the usual twelve. My last quarter, I was able to take a number of credits towards my master's degree, so I graduated with nine credits toward my master's plus my bachelor's in ten quarters, which I did by taking extra courses and by testing out of some of the basic subjects. Every quarter I could cut off was that much less money I had to raise.

I did go back on a half-time teaching scholarship to get my master's degree in the fifth year—I taught half-time and went to school half-time. I also did a research project in the summer on the farm, so I was out of MSU in thirteen terms with a master's degree, having taught half-time the last three terms.

Coming home to farm with a master's degree, I earned the fabulous wage of $250 a month. Clara and I, who by then had three children with a fourth on the way, rented a house from my cousin Raymond Carroll for thirty-five dollars a month.

Farming was not making Dad all that much money. He promised us a bonus if we would work with him not only on the farm but in marketing the fruit at the Eastern Farmers Market in Detroit in the fall. After Clara and I spent the entire fall working, that bonus turned out to be fifty dollars, which he gave Clara one morning in December as our Christmas present.

We weren't getting ahead quite as fast as we would have liked, but Dad had promised to start us up in farming. We were looking forward to getting a farm, and with possibly a teaching job on the side, we hoped to have the kind of steady income it would take to raise a family.

Originally the farm Dad promised me was the old Schafer place on East Bay, which joined our home farm on the peninsula on the east end. This 120 acres, north and south, included 3,900 feet of East Bay frontage, which nobody cared about in 1948 and '49.

We were interested in forty acres on a hill on the middle of the farm that was a nice- looking site for growing sour cherries. We figured we'd plant forty acres of cherries and have another sixty acres suitable for pasturing cattle. A small creek originated on the back end of our home farm and ran through the Schafer place and down to the bay; this would provide water for the cattle and we could pasture them there. Dad said he would buy this place for me, but it was in an estate. He said he'd pay the estate $8,500 for the 120 acres as soon as we got our cherries harvested in 1948.

Well, Les Jamieson, a neighbor of ours, was a little bit better off than we were. He and his wife were fruit farmers on the peninsula but also schoolteachers up on Drummond Island. Les wanted to set his brother Bud up in farming, so he went in the spring of the year (he had the money *before* the cherries were harvested) and bought the 120 acres for $6,500, including the 3,900 feet of East Bay frontage. I can still recall when Les decided to sell off the south four hundred feet on that place in four one hundred-foot lots at the fantastic price of ten dollars a foot, or one thousand dollars a lot. I remember Dad saying who in the hell would pay a thousand dollars for that pile of rocks, because the shore was somewhat rocky along there. Well, he lived long enough to see that lots of people were happy to pay a thousand dollars for one hundred feet of East Bay frontage. Anyway, that ended any possibility of me getting that farm. Land on the peninsula was difficult to come by, so we'd have to find property elsewhere.

Dad had noticed when he'd courted my mother that the Zimmermans had five acres of cherries on a knoll just east of Grandpa Fromholz' place in East Bay Township on Garfield Road. He said they had cherries most every time the peninsula did, so he felt that would be a suitable piece of ground. Zimmerman had retired and sold that 120 acres to my uncle, Harold Fromholz, for seven thousand dollars in 1948, but Uncle Harold now felt he needed more land and a house. Zimmerman had kept the house and three acres and just sold the farm and barn. Since Uncle Harold needed a house, he was interested in buying the Eikey farm on Potter Road. In order to come up with the down payment, he wanted to sell the Zimmerman farm, so he offered the 120 acres for twelve thousand dollars. My dad countered with an offer of ten thousand dollars and ended up buying it for eleven thousand dollars in 1951.

He then set out two blocks of cherries. In 1951 he planted 1,750 Montmorency cherry trees and the next year another two thousand. I was in college at the time, but my brother Frank was home on the farm and they set out those acreages along with caring for Dad's land on the peninsula. John Lyons, who lived in our neighborhood on the peninsula, also had forty acres of orchard just to the north of the Zimmerman piece. It wasn't unusual for peninsula farmers to buy land in other parts of the county and farm it along with what they had out on the gold coast.

Dad always said he would sell me that place, and in 1955 we finally settled on his price, which was thirty thousand dollars. That kind of floored me, but that's what he had into the land, the trees, the interest, and taxes. He said he would sell me that 120 acres with the forty acres of orchard for thirty thousand dollars, with the interest only at six percent for five years and the principal payable over the next twenty-five years. He was going to do it and going to do it and going to do it, but he wasn't getting it done very fast. One day when we were in town, walking up Union Street by what was the Traverse City State Bank, I said to him, "Let's go up to the lawyer's office and get them papers made out."

There wasn't much he could do except agree, so up we went. The lawyer we saw was Robert P. Griffin, who ended up a federal senator and eventually a Michigan Supreme Court justice, but at that time he was doing business out of his office in the Traverse City State Bank building. We made a contract and bought the place, Clara and I.

We were living on the peninsula and didn't have a house of our own, but we were talking about building a basement house on that farm. Then Zimmerman died and his old house and three acres went into an estate. He had four heirs and they wanted twelve thousand dollars for the house and the three and one-half acres that went with it that contained the Garfield Road frontage. (Originally, the 120-acre farm itself didn't have any Garfield Road frontage. Uncle Harold, during the time he owned it, had obtained twenty feet off my Grandpa Fromholz' farm, which gave him access to Garfield Road.) We didn't have the money to pay twelve thousand dollars for the old farmhouse, but I was interested. With all the kids Clara and I already had, we needed a big house and a lot of bedrooms and I didn't like the idea of having a basement house.

The house was purchased by Albert Rakowski, my mother's first cousin, son of Auntie (Antoinette Limburger) Rakowski, my grandmother Frances (Limburger) Fromholz' sister. Albert lived there when we were starting our operation. Eventually his wife died and he wanted to sell and move to Traverse City. I still wanted to buy the house, but my dad didn't want me to invest in a house—he thought that was a complete waste. He always pointed out to me that when the old German farmers came to this country, they always built a big barn and lived in whatever they could until they got the money together to build a real house. He said a farm and a barn would always build a house, but a house would never pay for a farm and a barn. He was probably right, but I needed the house, and I also thought it made sense to put this particular house and acreage back together like before.

I went out to talk to Albert one night. I had $250 in my bank account and Albert wanted eleven thousand dollars. I decided I wanted the house for eight thousand dollars. We started talking about seven o'clock in the evening, dickering back and forth. It was getting pretty close to eleven o'clock and I was still at eight thousand dollars, while Albert was down to $8,500. He finally looked at me and said, "I'm not going to sell you this house for eight thousand dollars."

I said, "Well, all right, let's split the difference and I'll give you $8,250 for it."

He said, "We've got a deal."

Now I had to scare up the money. I had the $250, but I needed eight thousand more. An elderly lady farmer by the name of Clara Douglas lived over on the southwest side of Traverse City, south of the state hospital, on some of that good land in the Lada neighborhood. She'd had the Cronenweth farms for many years. A very hard-working person, she had accumulated a few dollars and financed different farmers and others getting started for the interest. She had lent my Uncle Harold the money to buy the 120 acres, and at the time my dad bought that from him, she had a mortgage on it for $6,200, so I thought she was a logical person to borrow the money from. Since she had the money in the farm, maybe she'd be willing to lend me the money to buy the house.

Clara and I went together and told her we wanted that house. She listened to our story, then said, "That's a good house. I was there when they finished building it." This was apparently about 1909. They'd thrown a party, kind of a housewarming dance, which she'd attended. "Let me go in the bedroom and see how much money I've got on hand." She went into the bedroom, and when she came out she said, "I've only got seven thousand. You'll have to find the other thousand someplace else."

I went to my dad and said I wanted to borrow a thousand dollars from him against the wages I'd have coming in the summer and he said all right, so we had a house. It was in kind of bad shape when we got it. There was a porch across the front and some of the old posts were rotted out. Of course, the minute we bought it, before we moved in, my mother-in-law, my mother, and my cousins all came with scrub brushes and scrubbed the place from the attic through to the basement.

Over the years, we've made a lot of changes. We had to re-roof it eventually, and we had to insulate the whole thing and put on new drywall and we changed the rooms around and so on, but it's been a very good house to raise nine kids in, and it tied in very well with the farm.

Our home, built in 1909 of native brick from the Beitner yard, along with native stone from the farm

Ever since I was about sixteen, deer hunting has been a favorite sport of mine. In our youth, my cousin Jack Gallagher had a 30/40 Krag rifle and I borrowed a 32 Special from my Uncle Carl McManus. We each got a license and hunted in the Five Mile area of East Bay Township, which was all woods then. The last day of hunting season we were successful in getting a small buck—both of us shot at it simultaneously!

I decided to do some hunting over at the ranch in Kalkaska that my dad and Oliver Thompkins had bought called the Old Ingraham Ranch near Sharon. They pastured cattle on it in the summer and there were a lot of deer in that area. I hunted there for a few years until I got in college and then I had to give it up for a time.

After I got out of college, I was too busy to hunt for a while, but in 1958 Art Glidden, a very good friend of mine and the County Extension Director in Grand Traverse County who was largely responsible for me working for extension in the first place, asked if I wanted to join the Cedar Camp group of hunters he hunted with. One of their members, Ralph Coulter, had retired from extension and moved to Boulder, Colorado, and they needed another hunter to round out the group of six who hunted in the northern part of Menominee County in the Upper Peninsula each fall.

This was a great opportunity for me, as this group kept their costs low. They always prided themselves on not spending more than a hundred dollars each on their entire hunting excursion, including food, travel, and so on. This was accomplished by buying all their groceries wholesale rather than buying prepared foods or going out to eat. In the early days, we used wood for fuel, cooked on a wood stove, and used kerosene lamps. More recently we went to gas, but by staying in camp most of the time or spending our time in the woods, costs stayed low.

The group I originally went with consisted of Art Glidden (the county extension director from Grand Traverse County), Stanley Ball (the county extension director in Leelanau County), Russell Johnson (who at that time was with the Farmers Home Administration located in Petoskey; prior to that he had been an extension agent), Wilton Finley (a beef cattle specialist at Michigan State University and formerly the county extension director in Iosco County), Bill Murphy (the county extension director at Mount Clemens), and me.

Before that, the group included an extension agent by the name of McCarthy from over near Midland. They'd all hunted together since the late '30s and through World War II in such places as Brevort Lake and up north of Baraga. Just prior to my coming into the camp, they had hunted at Northland.

In 1956, Mr. Everett Stebbins owned a couple thousand acres at the north end of Menominee County near the Ford River, just south of Helps off Highway 569, and he invited the group to come hunt on his property, which we did until 2006, when the camp finally closed.

The Stebbins hauled what had been used as a logging camp up at Northland (originally a horse stable) down to a location on the west end of their property, added a small room for a so-called bedroom, and cedar-shingled the outside. That was the camp, essentially a T-shaped building. It was very small by most standards and was your typical boar's nest "Palace in the Popples." It was a great place, not only for hunting but for lots of philosophizing and discussions about how the extension service, state government, national government, the U.N., and most anything else that might come to mind should be run.

In the early days we had two woodstoves in the building, one for cooking in the so-called kitchen and a small box stove in the bedroom. The kitchen consisted of a stove, a cupboard for the dishes, a table for eating, and a small area for sitting around in the evening. Stanley Ball played the clarinet, Reuben Kaarre (who got in the camp later) played the violin, and Einer Olstrom played the harmonica.

In the early days, Finley brought kerosene lamps and we used to play cards in the evening. The camp was tight enough that after a while the lights would begin to dim as the oxygen lowered in the room. We'd have to open the door and let some air in to bring the lights back to full power. We watched that very carefully!

Camp wasn't too bad if the temperatures stayed reasonable. One year, the temperature was twenty degrees below zero the second morning of the season. That was a pretty cold one! Frost sat on all the nail heads in the ceiling and the walls, with a ring of frost around the inside of the building. It was much too cold to sit in the woods. That morning, Finley came back to camp about 9:00 a.m. and announced he'd crossed a bear track, so we spent the day tracking a bear through the swamps. We didn't get him, but we believe we got fairly close at different times. We hunted him as much to keep warm as for the possibility of finding him!

I was always the breakfast cook, making pancakes, eggs, bacon, fruit juice, and coffee. Glidden was always the dinner cook, and he cooked up a number of very good meals. Not only did he cook, he baked. Art loved preparing the meals as much as he loved hunting, and we had everything from roast turkey to steaks.

I also made baked fish annually with a recipe I brought from home. A lot of people don't know baked fish. In the U.P. you're able to get herring, which is the best, but you can't always get that south of the bridge, so we often ended up with Menominee. What you do is buy fresh Menominee and remove the bones. If you buy the whole fish, you finger bone it, which means slipping the bones out with your fingers, or you can buy the filets already boned. Take the filets, make sure you remove all the scales and fins, and marinate the flesh in wine for a day or at least part of a day, which tightens up the meat. Drain that off and put the fish in a baking dish with a little oil on the bottom to keep it from sticking, add some sliced onions in between, sprinkle on salt and pepper, and cover the whole thing with a couple of cans of mushroom soup. Bake it until it's done, then put some crumbed crackers on top and bake it just for a few minutes until they crisp up. It's an excellent dish with boiled potatoes and a vegetable. We usually had that once a year in camp.

For lunch, we usually just ate cheese and crackers or snacks or whatever leftovers we had from the night before. Once in a while we made a little soup. The total grocery bill for our ten days of camp was usually about forty dollars each.

We built a woodshed later on so we could cut wood a year ahead and stack it so it would be dry. There was an outside toilet, a two-holer. Our water supply consisted of a culvert that stood on end, placed in the ground about seven or eight feet. Roger Stebbins took a bulldozer years ago and bulldozed down to the bedrock (about five feet) and put the culvert in and filled in around it. The water would soak in and could be dipped by a pail on the end of a stick, the same way we used to dip water out of a cistern at my grandparents' place. We didn't use that water for drinking or cooking or making coffee. We brought water in with us or went to another camp to a drilled well and got fresh water for those purposes.

Later on we built a sauna for $123.00. There was room enough for three guys to get in at once. It had a stove with the typical stones on top. Reuben Kaare welded it up. We used five-gallon buckets for water, using one of them for a shower head so we could take a sauna and then shower off. That was a great addition to camp!

Eventually the campers changed and different people came in. Bill MacLean, the horticultural agent from Oceana County, hunted with us for a while and then quit, Murphy passed on, and then we went to eight campers. Einer Olstrom, one of the administrators in the extension service who had formerly been a 4-H agent, joined us, and then a former county director over in Missaukee County who was located in East Lansing came on board. Reuben Kaarre, a county extension director in Ogemaw County, came in, and Warren Cook, who at the time he came into camp was a county extension director in Kalkaska County but ended up down at Charlotte, joined us. Glidden eventually passed out of the picture and so did Ball and Finley until Russell Johnson and I were the only two of that original group left.

Eventually, Mr. Stebbins decided to clear-cut a lot of the area around camp. Even though the building was somewhat rustic and primitive, camp had been in a beautiful secluded location with pines and popples (aspen) and other species of trees at the end of a long trail in the woods where you could hear coyotes at night.

After the land around it was cleared, camp looked pretty barren and that changed things. It discouraged some of the fellows from hunting, and others got various ailments and were no longer able to do it, so a third set of hunters came in. Steve Fouch, the county ag agent in Benzie County, and Mark Ash from over in Cheboygan County became part of the group, along with George Bumgartner, one of the building inspectors in Emmet County, and his son-in-law and one of his co-workers. John McKinney, the marine agent at Traverse City, came into the camp several years back, making a group of eight once again.

Even though we took many bucks out of that area, you have to take the attitude when you deer hunt that you can have a successful hunt without getting a deer. I guess I probably averaged getting a buck about half the time. The camaraderie, the discussions, and the philosophy generated at noon and in the evening and even sometimes in the morning after breakfast added a real dimension to everyone's lives, particularly those of us in public service.

The other valuable aspect of hunting is the privilege of being in the woods in a solitary and beautiful environment where you can walk through various swamps and over ridges and down trails and get a look at nature in the raw. There's lots of time for meditation when you're sitting on a stump waiting for Mr. Buck to come by. You think about the previous year's activities and the responsibilities coming up for the next year. Hunting camp is therapeutic. It gets you away from the telephone and all the modern conveniences and takes you back to the simple life, or life as it was in the raw many years ago.

The biggest buck I ever got at camp was a seventeen-pointer, or at least I counted it as a seventeen-pointer. Some people counted it a fifteen-pointer because of the side antler that came from the main rack with a couple of points on it. I well remember the day in 1978. I had been in my blind all morning; we usually hunted until 12:00 and then joined a couple of other hunters to go back to camp for lunch. It was 12:00 and I decided I was going to wait an extra five minutes to see if anything came in. A little doe came up the trail, looking behind her and acting rather nervous, and I thought this was kind of interesting.

What I expected was a small spike horn or four point, but what came walking towards me had such a huge rack of antlers, it was almost a brush pile. After I shot him, the buck ran a little ways into the woods, but not far. Then one of the other boys came over and helped me drag him out. I had the head and the rack, the whole thing, mounted.

Hunting is a great sport. There's much more to it than just shooting a deer. People who have hunted the same place for years get to know their territory almost as well as they know their own farm or land, and different features in the geography get names like Apple Ridge, Gravel Pit, Crow Corner, Old Baldy, the Island, Duane's Hardwoods, and so on. Crow Corner has been called that since 1958 because of the dead crow found in the road about 1956. Apple Ridge is so called because Bill Finley used to put out apples for the deer there, which the squirrels also ate.

Even better, venison is an excellent food because it doesn't have a lot of fat and you usually trim off whatever fat there is before cooking it. I think venison is probably best eaten right in camp. We usually made a couple of meals, with the first guy to get a buck agreeing to give up a portion of it to the camp. We'd take out a hind quarter and usually have one meal, possibly two, of venison steak.

Warren Cook probably had the best system of cooking venison steak. He'd slice the meat and pound flour into it, then boil up the potatoes and other things until they were ready, then put some griddles on the stove and get them good and hot. He'd put butter on the griddles and fry the venison just until it was done on each side and immediately serve it, hot off the griddle. Quite often we took a grinder to camp and ground up some of the venison for chili, too, and when we got home, we'd cut up our deer and freeze it for use during the coming year.

I especially like to cook a venison roast. I learned my method from Edna Alsup, our home demonstration agent, many years ago. You put the roast in aluminum foil and add a half or three-quarters cup of black coffee to another half to three-quarters cup of red wine. Mix it all together with a little onion on top, add salt and pepper, pour it all on the roast, seal the aluminum foil, and bake in the oven until done.

A certain amount of leg-pulling always goes on in hunting camp. The first year I hunted with the group in the U.P, they used to go to town once during the season for dinner. In those days we Catholics couldn't eat meat on Fridays. A couple of the guys, Glidden and Ball, started talking about going to town for a meal "the day after tomorrow" and we all agreed. It didn't occur to me this would be Friday, because we never paid any attention to what day of the week it was in deer camp. Our camp was thirty-five miles from downtown Escanaba. We got in the car that night and headed out. About halfway there, when it was too late to turn back, somebody said, "What day of the week is this?"

Someone else said, "Oh, it's Friday."

Some of us thought, "Uh oh, we've been had. They'll all get steak and we'll have to eat fish."

The group wanted to go to Skinny's Bar in Escanaba. When we got there, the waitress said they had perch on special that night. Murphy,

Finley, and McManus said they'd have the perch. Art Glidden kind of eased back in his chair and said, "What else do you have?"

She said, "Whitefish, trout, or shrimp. We don't serve any meat on Friday."

So we all had the perch. We talked about that many, many times afterwards! The history of this camp and group of hunters may be found in the archives at Michigan State University under the title "Cedar Camp History" by John McKinney.

I never did a lot of other hunting in life. Usually after a week of deer hunting in the U.P., I'd come back to the farm, put the gun away, and hang up the hunting clothes for another year. I didn't bother to hunt on my own land. We always left our land open for the neighbors to hunt, and by the time I got back from camp, they had the deer either hunted or chased out.

I did have a 12-gauge shotgun when I was a teenager and I did some squirrel hunting and a bit of rabbit hunting. I also once went pheasant hunting with John Bray, an extension agent who worked for Michigan State when I did. He lived over in the thumb area in Saginaw County and he invited me to go pheasant hunting with him at a time when Michigan had pheasants to hunt. We had one or two seasons of that before John moved, but my hunting has been primarily deer each year. It's an annual trek to the woods as well as a hunt. I could easily hunt at home if getting a deer was all I was after.

Talking about hunting, I don't know if many in the younger generation have heard of snipe hunting, but when I was a young teenager, I was up to my grandparents' place one day after supper when my Uncle Carl asked me if I wanted to go snipe hunting. I was all ears, and of course very interested. I asked, "What's a snipe?"

"A small bird," he said. "It's a . . . "

"How do you hunt them?" I was excited!

"Get a gunny sack and a couple of sticks and come with me."

He took me down to a secluded place in the woods not too far from the house, maybe a thousand feet or two, and said, "You sit here and hold the bag and rub those sticks together periodically. I'll go down to the other end of the woods and round the snipe up and drive them back your way. When they come, if you rub them sticks, they'll go right into the bag."

I sat there and held the bag thirty minutes . . . forty-five minutes . . . then an hour . . . then an hour and a half. Finally it started to get dark. I decided something was wrong, so I yelled a couple of times for my uncle. I didn't get any response, so finally I walked on back to the house. When I got to my grandparents' house, my uncle said, "Did you see any?" I said, "No, I didn't see any." He kind of giggled and all of a sudden I knew I'd been had, and I guess that wasn't the last time I was left "holding the bag."

Chapter Six
Language, Nationality, Religion, and All That Came with It

One of the interesting points that should come out in any family history is how language changes over the years. Some of the words my Irish ancestors used when they first came to the peninsula in the middle 1800s were quite different from the language we speak today. One of the most interesting words they used was the word "aye," pronounced "I." Today we usually say "yes." If my granddad acknowledged something that he agreed with, he would say "aye" in a monotone. At the same time, if he questioned something, he used the word "aye" with a rising inflection at the end, drawing in his breath at the same time—like "ha-aye." I've never seen or heard that out of the present generation or my father's generation, but I've heard it in Ireland; it's definitely a hand-me-down from the Irish.

My granddad also used the word "sayed" for the past tense of "say" instead of "said." For instance, when he was talking about his dad, he would say, "Paw [he always called his dad "Paw" and his mother "Maw"] sayed" and then he'd go on to explain what his dad had said.

Likewise, he always used the word "twas" in place of "it was." He'd say, "Paw sayed twas" and finish his sentence. When he said "The Lord's Prayer," he always used the word "t'is" as in "One earth as t'is in heaven."

When he was hauling something, he'd say "drawed," as in "we drawed" water from the spring." He used the word "fetch" sometimes, but more often "drawed."

I never heard my granddad swear. Grandpa Fromholz was pretty good at it, but Granddad McManus would say "By jinx" if he wanted to express himself strongly. "By jinx, it t'is or t'isn't" and so on. It was a different variation of the English we use today.

Great-grandma Mcmanus was a very devout Catholic in her own way, as was my grandfather, her son, although I never realized it too much at the time. Grandpa was a pretty tough old character. He loved to play cards, he was a hard worker, and he never spoke a lot about religion, but thinking back over how he did things, I'd have to conclude he was actually quite religious. He attended church regularly, walking the two miles from his house to church in the early days, partly to attend services, partly to think, and partly to stop on the way back and visit with his mother some because she lived about halfway in between church and home.

I can remember a custom he had during Lent. We would go to his place to play cards at night, and after supper, before we were allowed to start a game, we'd go into the living room and everyone would turn their chairs around and kneel on the floor with our elbows on the seat and Grandpa would lead the Rosary. I never thought about it much until later in life, but I got to talking to my aunts about it and they said, "Oh yes, he was very particular about certain kinds of devotions." During Lent they had to say the Rosary every night after supper before they could play. If they were going ice skating or playing any kind of sport or cards or anything else, they always had to say the Rosary first.

One of my Dad's best friends, and probably one of the men he respected most in life, was a Catholic priest named Father Kyran McGinn. McGinn was a tall, likeable Irishman. He liked to play basketball with the boys and was a friendly, affable fellow. My dad was quite an athlete and they got to be good friends. One of the stories he told about McGinn is that they went to a ball game in Traverse City one night. McGinn had his Roman collar on and they were sitting in the stands when a couple of local gentry decided to poke fun at McGinn. They were sitting behind him and they kept talking about the collar he had on turned around backwards. McGinn took it for quite a while and finally, when he got tired of it, turned around and said, "Now boys, if that collar is botherin' you all that bad, we'll step out there behind the stands and I'll take it off and we'll see how much it really troubles you." That was the last they heard about the collar.

One of the most interesting events in my dad's life, of course, was marrying my mother. Dad was from a big poor Irish family on the peninsula and my mother was from a German family a little bit higher up on the economic pole in East Bay Township. She was the oldest of a family of five, a full-blooded German, and her parents were German Lutheran, so we had a situation where an Irish Catholic wanted to marry a German Lutheran. Worse yet, Grandma Fromholz was actually a fallen-away Catholic who had left the faith when she was a young girl. Her ancestors were from the southern part of Germany, while Grandpa Fromholz' ancestors were from the northern part. Grandma Fromholz had left the church when she was about fifteen years old, apparently over some kind of argument in the confessional.

She lived out in the country on the farm and hadn't been to church from Christmas until Easter. She got to church late that Easter and walked into the confessional and told the priest she hadn't been to church for that period of time. He proceeded to bawl her out pretty bad. She thought everybody in church could hear, so when she walked out of that confessional, she never went back.

She didn't want her oldest daughter to marry down and get involved in the Catholic Church. At first she threatened to take my mother to Germany. She'd inherited some money when her mother died and she was going to take Ma to Germany and get this idea of wedding an Irishman out of her mind, but that didn't transpire. My mother didn't want to go anyway, so Grandma decided on another plan. She had enough familiarity with the Catholic Church to know that if you were Catholic, you married another Catholic and you got married in church, or if it was a Catholic marrying a Protestant (what's known as a mixed marriage), you got married in the rectory. She figured she could put a stop to the wedding if she insisted it take place at her home, so she announced to my dad and mother that if they were going to get married, they'd have to do it at her home on Garfield Road next door to where I live today.

The next Sunday, my dad went to Mass in the morning. Afterwards, he went up to see his friend, Father McGinn. McGinn said, "What do you need, Mack?" My dad's friends always called him "Mack."

Dad told him he wanted to marry this little German girl and he was having a problem with her mother. McGinn asked what kind of problem and Dad replied, "The old lady insists that it be in her living room."

"Well," McGinn said, "If it's in the parlor she wants the wedding, in the parlor it'll be, and I'll be there."

My dad said, "Do you mean it?"

"Certainly. I'll perform the wedding there."

That made my dad's day. He went out to the Fromholz house for Sunday dinner and they got around to the subject of the wedding. Grandma said it had to be in the parlor and Dad said that would be fine, that Father McGinn would be there to perform the ceremony.

Grandma said, "Priests don't do that. They don't come to people's houses to marry them."

My dad said, "This one will."

So the wedding was held, and Grandmother Fromholz always prided herself afterwards. Anytime anybody asked about it, she said, "The priest had to come to my house." She never gave in!

An interesting sequel to the story is that after the plans were made, my dad told his parents he was marrying Frieda and that the wedding was going to be at the Fromholz home. His mother said his father, who was a pretty strong Catholic and Irish to boot, wouldn't attend, and my dad asked why.

"Well, the wedding won't be performed by the priest."

"Yes it is," my dad said. "McGinn's going to do it."

"Your father doesn't know that. You'd better talk to him."

Grandpa was hoeing corn. Whenever he didn't have anything else to do, he was always hoeing something. My dad said he was getting married and understood that Grandpa wasn't going to attend the ceremony.

Grandpa said, "Yep, that's right."

My dad said, "Well, that'll be all right. Whatever you want to do. But we're having the wedding out at Fromholz' house, and McGinn's going to do the job."

Grandpa just cleared his throat with a harrumph and said, "Priests don't go into a house to marry nobody."

"Have it your own way," my dad said, "but he's agreed to do it and he'll be performin' the wedding."

So Grandpa McManus showed up and McGinn performed the ceremony and everything went along according to plan. I bring this up because when I was a boy, we had to learn our catechism in the Catholic Church. Father Schultz was the pastor at Elk Rapids with a mission at Mapleton where I attended. When we went for first communion, he taught the catechism and the various instructions. At the same time, a common practice in our family was to go to the Fromholzes every Sunday for dinner. The Protestant Sunday School was held in the Haney School, about half a mile down the road. We'd go to Mass at Mapleton at 8:30 a.m. and then out to Grandma Fromholz's for dinner. She'd give Frank and me each a penny and we'd have to go to Haney and get the Protestant version of Sunday school, so you might say I was brought up in both churches. Many of the old hymns in the Protestant Church that I learned in my youth are very near and dear to me still.

The little log church that sits in Old Mission today is a replica of the one Reverend Peter Dougherty, the Scottish minister, founded. His was the first church on the peninsula. At the time I was a boy, there was also a Congregational Church at Old Mission, a Methodist Church at Ogdensburg, and the Catholic Church, St. Joseph's, at Mapleton. In my boyhood, St. Joseph's was a mission of the mother church at Elk Rapids. Before that, it was a mission of St. Francis of Traverse City. Having the mother church at Elk Rapids in the early days was more convenient—it enabled the priests to come across the bay by boat in the summertime and across the ice in the winter. For many, many years, the Mapleton church was connected to the Elk Rapids mother parish. Elk Rapids had two missions, actually, one at Barker Creek (now St. Mary's Church in Kalkaska) as well as St. Joseph's Church at Mapleton. St. Joseph's was transferred back to St. Francis eventually and became a parish of its own, as it remains today.

Father Stratz was the first pastor I knew. My first communion instructions were by Father Schultz back in the 1930s. He was followed by Father Sikorski, then Father Winikaitis, and many, many others up to Father Frederick and beyond. There were a lot of Irish in the parish, but also Bohemians and others. The Carrolls, McManuses, Buchans, and Swaneys were Irish. So were the Boursaws through their mother, but the Kroupas were Bohemian. There were also other nationalities and mixtures, though not a lot of French, surprisingly.

Religion always played a big part in my life and in the lives of other members of our family. We were raised Roman Catholic, and the McManuses have belonged to St. Joseph's Catholic Church at Mapleton since it was originally built. The Carrolls (Grandmother McManus was a Carroll) have also been members since the beginning. So on my dad's side of the family, there was never much doubt as to what faith we were going to practice. Dad was a very strong Catholic in his own way. As far as instructions in the faith went, he probably had the usual week or two weeks of instructions sometime early on when he made his first communion. I don't know whether he was ever confirmed or not, but he was a strong defender of the faith and a pillar of the church. He was buried, as were his folks, in the Catholic cemetery on the peninsula.

My mother, on the other hand, remained a Lutheran until I was thirteen years old, though she did the job of giving my brother Frank and me our instructions and taught us our Baltimore Catechism as she had agreed to at the time she married my dad. My sister Antoinette, born in 1938, was raised Catholic too, as were my other siblings. Ma never attended the Lutheran Church after she married my dad. She probably didn't attend all that much beforehand. Once she was married and living on the peninsula, the closest Lutheran church was in Traverse City. She never made any particular move to attend services there, though she did carry her Lutheran Bible with her at the house until she died. She probably got that when she took catechism lessons in the Lutheran Church as a child.

My dad never asked her to join the Catholic Church. He always felt religion was a private matter for each individual. If she wanted to join, he would certainly welcome it, but he never put any pressure on her to do so. She probably waited as long as she did because her parents weren't Catholic and they were all pretty close-knit and she didn't want to offend them. She went to church every Sunday with us at St. Joe's in Mapleton from the earliest time I can remember, but she didn't join until 1943.

That probably came about for a couple of reasons. One, her brother Harold Fromholz, my uncle, was going with Dora Alpers, whom he eventually married. He made the decision to join the Catholic church at the time he married Dora. After he broke the ice, so to speak, I think Ma felt free to go ahead and do it, too.

Also, Father Winikaitas was the priest at Mapleton at the time she joined, and he was a kind of easygoing Lithuanian priest. In fact, he was so easygoing that periodically his plaid shirt collar would stick up above his Roman collar when he was saying mass. He liked to hunt and fish, and one time he got arrested by the conservation department for keeping an undersized fish. It even made the paper. Of course, George Lardie, who was married to Alberta McManus, was kind of a cut-up in Old Mission and he belonged to the church, too. He put a six-inch ruler in the collection plate the next Sunday for the good father, but Winikaitas took it pretty well.

Father Winikaitas was giving instructions for converts at about the time Ma decided to become Catholic. There were half a dozen people taking their instructions at the same time, and she felt comfortable discussing things with that particular group, including father.

I don't remember her joining, but people told me afterwards it was of the few times anybody ever saw my dad cry. He felt so joyful that she had joined up with him. But she came from a different background, so she was not a typical Catholic who was used to saying the Rosary and so on. She always had us say our prayers before we went to bed at night, but the Rosary wasn't familiar to her like it is to a lot of people who are brought up in the Catholic church. She didn't serve any meat on Friday, of course, but Latin and so on were a mystery to her. Nonetheless, Ma was internally a religious person and knew very well the difference between right and wrong and she taught us that whether she was Lutheran or Catholic. She was eventually buried in the Catholic cemetery at Mapleton with my dad.

The year she joined the church, I was in my first year at St. Francis. Sister Kathleen Bannon was the teacher in the eighth grade and she knew about it. I'd apparently told her. I remember her giving me kind of a pearl cross about five or six inches tall to give to my mother as a present for becoming a Catholic.

Our family always sat in the second pew from the back on the left hand side of the church as you walked in. Of course, in the early days everyone paid a two-dollar annual pew rent fee and sat in their own pew. It wasn't like it is today, where you sit wherever you feel like. We also had to pay attention during church. My dad had a system for keeping my brother and I well disciplined: if we got to horsing around, he'd reach over and take us by the nape of the neck and raise us up a little. It was embarrassing enough that we got the message and settled down.

At about the eighth grade level, we had to take instructions to become altar boys and learn the Latin prayers that go with the mass. I was an altar boy for several years. My brother Frank eventually was too, as well as my other brothers. Stanley Wood was in my age group and we served mass together for many years.

In the early days, that church was much smaller than it is today and the farmers and other members from the area would go to Mass the first and third Sundays of the month at 8:30, and the second and fourth and occasional fifth Sundays at 10:30, because the priest had to serve Elk Rapids and Mapleton and also Barker Creek. Only one Mass was offered per Sunday in each place and priests were limited on the numbers and times they could offer a Mass.

In those days, everybody sat in their cars in the parking area until the bell rang to signify the beginning of the service. Once it rang, everybody got out and went in. I didn't learn until I began attending church in Traverse City that you could go in anytime. In fact, you were expected to get in there a little early and not come in at the last minute. Until then, I thought you had to wait until the bell rang before you got out of the car and went inside, unless confession was offered and you needed to go.

Confession was sometimes held before mass and at Lenten services, usually on Wednesday nights. We'd have stations of the cross, and one time I remember they had kind of a question period during Lent. It was an instructional part of the session and you could write questions and put them in a box and the priest would try to answer them. I remember somebody wondering if it would be okay to eat meat on Good Friday if it fell on Easter Sunday. The priest answered yes, if Good Friday ever fell on Easter Sunday, it would be okay to eat meat!

I was confirmed by Bishop Haas out of Grand Rapids. In those days, we were part of the Grand Rapids Diocese; the Gaylord Diocese was created much later. Normally people who were going to be confirmed had to go to Traverse City and be confirmed at St. Francis. A decision was made to have the bishop come out to the peninsula and confirm us there. This caused quite a to-do, because the steps going up to the altar were so narrow and steep there was concern about how everyone was going to get up and down without tripping, but we made it through all right and were confirmed in St. Joseph's church.

I eventually took some music. I was in the peninsula band when I was in the sixth and seventh grades and I learned enough to read the treble clef notes and play the cornet. My mother was a piano player who had taken music from Sister Cecilia in Traverse City many years before. She was a pretty good pianist, and she wanted me to learn to play piano. We took lessons, but we didn't have a piano to start with so we practiced on a keyboard that didn't have any sound. It wasn't very inspiring, but eventually we were able to get a used piano and Ma would play once in a while. My dad really enjoyed it when she sat down and played.

Ma's family's love of music didn't carry down very well in our family. Grandpa Fromholz played the harmonica and both my German grandparents loved singing and dancing. I probably should have kept it up more myself, but somehow I didn't follow through all that well. I took piano lessons at St. Francis in the eighth grade and again in the ninth and I could read the bass clef, but not as fast as I could read the treble clef, so it was always difficult for me to play anything very complicated.

The Basilion Hymnals we used were fairly simple, with a couple of the notes on the treble clef and a couple on the bottom, though sometimes three on top. I could play that and I eventually got to be the organist in the Mapleton Church. It was a pump organ, the old kind where you pump the air into the bellows with both of your feet and the volume is controlled by a pedal with the knees. We also had the keyboard and the stops, which determined what kind of combination of sounds came out.

I was the organist for several years, through high school and college and beyond. Eventually a Wurlitzer electric organ was purchased for the fabulous sum of $1,100. I remember they thought they wanted an electric and that was some improvement over the old system. I understand they've since bought something a little more sophisticated than that particular instrument, but that's how we got by for several years.

Transferring to St. Francis in the eighth grade was a major move. Coming from my tiny church at Mapleton, St. Francis looked huge. I didn't realize until many years later how small it actually was because it was so many times bigger than my home church and so much more elaborately decorated, with colored windows and much larger stations of the cross. The windows in my church were just frosted glass, even though most Catholic churches in those days had colored windows of some sort. St. Francis even had pictures of the saints, a high altar in the back, and a much larger communion railing with an altar cloth that the altar boys flipped over before communion began. On top of that, they had a brilliant pipe organ imported from Austria back in the 1800s that fit the size of the church so that the music was the grandest I'd ever heard.

In addition, they had four bells on rockers that were rung just before mass, while Mapleton had just one bell.

At St. Francis, I was introduced to the high mass, which was sung in Latin with the Gloria and the Credo and the Agnus Dei and the Kyrie. I was also introduced to the Angelus. The bells at St. Francis were rung at six a.m., at noon, and at six p.m. for the Angelus each day. We never had that at Mapleton; we'd never even heard of it. The crowds were also much larger at St. Francis and schoolchildren always sang the masses at funerals. We were also introduced to novenas and retreats. We got lots of exposure at St. Francis, more by far that we'd had at Mapleton.

It was unfortunate that the people who built St. Francis in 1887 didn't have enough money to use brick. As such, the old wooden church eventually had to be torn down and a new church built, which of course meant a completely different type of architecture.

The old Gothic church was a beautiful thing, in my estimation. It resembled the churches in southern Germany with its very high steeple and belfry. It used to be one of the main features of the skyline in Traverse City. If you came into town from any of the surrounding hills or up the bay, you saw the Park Place Hotel, the Methodist Church, and the steeple of St. Francis. It was a major part of the town's architecture and it was a real loss when it had to come down.

The St. Francis Church in Petoskey, which is likewise a part of the skyline of that town, was built of brick and has been maintained. I must say, it has always distressed me that we spent time and effort to preserve buildings like the City Opera House and the state hospital buildings but were not able to figure how to preserve a building that was very important to settlers from the early days of Traverse City on, but so goes the world.

St. Francis originally had a furnace in the basement that used wood and later coal; eventually it was heated from the furnace located at the school. Clara's ancestors on her mother's side helped to build that church. It was well built, because even after it had sat unused for a few years, it looked pretty good. It had deteriorated by the time they came with the crane to hit the steeple and tear it down, but the first time the iron ball hit the steeple, it just bounced back, so the building was well constructed.

When I was in school, a wooden school faced Cass Street with a grade school on the first floor and the high school on the second floor. An annex was used for the grade school and was tied into an auditorium or gymnasium with a stage we could use for basketball or band or putting on school plays or meetings.

The same property housed the convent that was also built back in the late 1800s. The wooden part of it was the mother house of the Dominican Order that came from Regensburg, Germany, in the 1880s to teach school and housed their postulants and sisters. It became a boarding school for a while, but eventually was used only for housing the nuns. St. Francis was the oldest mother house of the Dominicans in Michigan to start with. The school began on Union Street, but eventually moved to Tenth Street. It consisted of a convent, a chapel, and a boarding school. There was originally a covered walkway between the convent and the school and the convent and the church so the sisters could maintain part of their cloistered activities and stay undercover, as we'd put it today, rather than be out in public.

In the original church, above the altar on the right and left sides, were balconies with grilled windows in front. In the early days of the 1900s, the sisters came from the convent up to the church and into those balconies to attend mass behind those grilled windows, much the same as the Carmelites do today. When they went to communion, they came down the stairs as far as the door into the sanctuary and were given communion there. They were not part of the congregation.

By the time I got there in 1945, all that had changed. The grilled windows were plastered over and the nuns had their own church at the convent, but when they did attend at St. Francis, they attended this part of the congregation.

Piano lessons were given at the convent. One room had two grand pianos so we could play duets with another practice room in the convent as well. The sisters also had a chapel made of brick on the east end of the building about the same size inside as the Mapleton Church. It was kind of a small chapel, but it was big enough to seat twenty sisters, with extra seats for the congregation. I served mass there with Stanley Wood one time when I was in high school.

As we went through school, we took religion as a separate subject each year. Church history was one subject, and the last two years we moved into philosophy, which got a little complicated. All in all, we picked up a lot of information about the Bible and church doctrine and also church organization.

I graduated from St. Francis High School, as did my sisters Antoinette and Frieda. My four brothers all graduated from Traverse City Public School, but Frank and Art did have a few years at St. Francis. Because we were from the Mapleton parish, we had to pay tuition to attend St. Francis. At the time I went, my dad paid fifteen dollars for one child and twenty-five dollars for two.

My grandmother McManus had attended the convent boarding school in the late 1800s, so she was quite insistent I attend that particular school. My dad had been kicked out in the 1920s so he wasn't too excited about it, but I met Clara there. She came over to St. Francis in the eleventh grade and we attended the last two years of high school together. I also attended the public school because St. Francis didn't teach physics and I wanted to take that course, so every day I walked over to the public school for that class.

I never thought too much about the unity of the Catholic church worldwide until the year Clara and I made a trip to Rome when our oldest daughter, Lisa Jane, was attending Loyola University in Rome and invited us over after Christmas. We spent several days in Rome and visited St. Peter's. I thought St. Francis was a big church, but when you get into St. Peter's, you realize you could fit St. Francis into one tiny corner. In fact, there's a brass marker on the floor of the main aisle in that church for the length of each of the major cathedrals in the world; none of them reaches the length of St. Peter's. Also, as you walk in, you're not impressed as much as you should be until you realize the ceiling is high enough that you could have two levels of statuary at their complete height plus add the room in between. It's a huge place.

We had a public audience in Rome with Pope Paul VI attended by people from all over the world. A couple of things really impressed me. One was the fact that the pope spoke to each different ethnic group in their native language. Of course it felt more like a football game with a cheering section than a church. As the pope came in, there was a lot of clapping, cheering, and yelling. It was not at all solemn initially, but then he got up in the front and talked in each language and at the end of the ceremony, we all sang the Credo in Latin. It was very inspiring to hear the various nationalities sing that song in Latin as they'd learned to do in their home churches and schools, the same as I had back in the eighth grade in St. Francis.

I often hear discussion on the topic of infallibility. Of course, if you follow church dogma closely, infallibility only pertains to certain dogma that the church proclaims and not to a whole lot of other things that are done in the name of Catholicism throughout the world. But the infallibility part of the doctrine pertains to some of the basic beliefs of the church and does not constitute the biggest percentage of various things that a lot of us do as we go through life. It always creates a great deal of consternation when people get into theological and philosophical discussions about whether or not the church and pope are infallible.

One of the best comments I ever heard on this subject came from an old nun I had in the eleventh grade. She said, "Well, the proof of infallibility of the Catholic Church is the fact that it's still running after two thousand years." She didn't actually say two thousand, because this was about 1940, but the church is still running today in spite of the people who've been in charge. I suppose that probably sums up a lot of theology in one short statement, regarding the works of the Holy Spirit.

Sometimes we hear a lot of criticism of religion because it's slow and onerous to understand, but probably it's a little bit like democracy, which is also slow and sometimes difficult to see through, but in both cases beats the alternative.

Periodically we also hear about the subject of separation of church and state. That's a longer discussion than I care to get into here, but an Irish priest I heard one time probably summed it up best when he said, "You talk about the separation of church and state. I sure hope they keep them separated, because if they ever put them together, they'd have the greatest collection of idiots known to man!"

Another story that perhaps came a little later in life is about the young priest who was assigned a church. He was a little nervous, so he said to the older priest he was assigned under, "How do you maintain your calm demeanor when you're giving a sermon so you don't become nervous?"

The old priest said, "Well, remember that glass of water on the lectern where we preach? That's really not water; it's gin. As I go along in my sermon, I take a little nip from time to time and that eases me over the nervousness I might otherwise feel."

The young priest decided that was a good idea and he'd try it out. The next Sunday, he came out after Mass and said to the old priest, "How did I do?"

The old priest said, "Pretty well, until you came to the part in the Bible about David and the Philistines. The passage correctly says, 'David slew ten thousand Philistines with the jawbone of an ass.' It doesn't say he chewed the ass out of ten thousand Philistines until he broke his jawbone!"

Since I'm on a roll, I'll tell a few more stories. Back in the 1960s, church doors were suddenly thrown open to any kind of activity or demeanor or dress. When I was young, ladies always dressed up rather formally to attend services. Many wore hats and everything was quite proper. But in the '60s, much of that was thrown out. One young lady came to church one Sunday morning about that time without anything on above the waist. When she came down for communion, the priest said, "I'm refusing you communion. You don't have any clothes on above the waist."

She said to him, "I have a divine right."

He said, "You've got a dandy left, too, but you still don't get any communion."

Another story that went around in the 1940s and '50s is about the priest in Ireland who was having trouble getting Pat to come to church. Pat was nippin' the bottle and not attending regularly, so the good father thought he should go talk to him and get him back to church.

He went out to Pat's farm and found him in the potato field hoeing away. The priest thought he'd use a little psychology, so he said, "Pat, that's a beautiful field of potatoes you and the Lord have here."

Pat looked back at him and said, "Yes, Father, it certainly is, but you should have seen this field when the Lord had it by himself!"

There's also the story about the fellow who came out of church one Sunday with two black eyes. He met his friend, who said, "How in the world did you get two black eyes goin' to church?"

"It was hot in there," the first fellow said. "When we were in church and it came time to stand up, the dress of the lady in front of me was caught between her legs. I knew she wouldn't want it that way, so I reached up and pulled her dress carefully out, and when she felt me doin' it, she hauled off and swung around with her purse and gave me a black eye."

His friend said, "How'd you get the second black eye?"

The first fellow said, "The next time we stood up, her dress hung down straight. I knew she must have wanted it tucked in, so I carefully pushed it in and that's when she swung around and gave me the second one."

Chapter Seven

My Childhood through the First Years of Marriage

I was born on December 12, 1930, on the Murray farm on the second floor of a two-story garage, formerly a carriage house, in the hired man's quarters. It's the third building north of the intersection of Montague Road and M-37 on the peninsula and it's still standing today. My dad worked on the farm and my mother originally worked in the house. I don't recall much about that time because I lived there before I was five years old, but I do remember the Murray kids, Benny, Davey, and Sally,(they had a brother Howard who died young also), having a nice playroom in their house with big wooden building blocks. They were a little bit like the lock-a-block toys we have nowadays, but these were much bigger and didn't have a locking mechanism.

My brother Frank was born on the Will Buchan farm. The Montagues inherited it after Bill Buchan died and a man by the name of Schultz eventually bought the farm. The house is on West Shore Road and is made of stone. Frank was born in an old tenant house away from the road a bit north and east of the barn in a little grove.

We almost lost Frank at birth. His thymus gland didn't close properly and it was touch and go for a few days. The doctor prescribed a drop of whiskey on the hour to keep him going.plus fresh air from keeping a window partly open near his crib(This was in December) He was a small baby, but the whiskey brought him through and Frank turned out to be a good husky lad who along with Leona has raised a sizeable family. Right now he's got more grandkids than I have.

My sister Antoinette was born in the car halfway up Carpenter Hill on the way to Traverse City to go the hospital. We were living at the Anderson farm just north of McKinley Road on the east side of the road because my dad worked some for Clarence Anderson. Dad had decided to draw a load of gravel from Wilson's gravel pit, which in those days was on the north side of Carpenter Hill as you came up the first hill on the peninsula. That's all been bulldozed together now and leveled up and those who haven't been around too long probably would never know it was there. Dad indicated he would be home at noon for dinner, but Mom started having labor pains in the morning. By the time he got home at noon, things were pretty far along. He got her right in the car and headed for town, but it was too late. He took Mom and the baby on into Munson anyway and everybody was fine.

Antoinette eventually went through Maple Grove School, then onto St. Francis. She married Ronnie Lints and they raised a sizeable family. Unfortunately, Antoinette was a smoker and developed cancer and died early in life at age forty-nine. She was a great sister and one we all continue to miss. She was kind of a mother to our younger brothers and sisters because our own mother died at fifty-three from kidney stones, when Pat and Mike and Frieda were still pretty young. Antoinette acted as a mother to those kids and did a very good job. I can't say enough good things about my sister and all the sacrifices she made for our family.

We moved in 1935 to our farm north of the Chateau Grand Traverse winery on the north side of Carroll Hill. When Art came along, he was named after his grandfather, while Mike was named after the Limburger side of the family. Then Pat and Frieda Ann came. Frieda, of course, was named after my mother. They were all born in Munson Hospital, in Traverse City.

The family has stayed in the Traverse City area, contrasted with many families of our size who have moved on to big cities for employment. All five of us boys have our finger in a farming operation in one way or another. Mike turned out to be a schoolteacher in the Traverse City school system for many years, and Pat was the only full-time farmer out of the bunch of us. Art worked for Consumers Power Company and Frank worked for a long time with the Traverse City Iron Works, although he's now retired. Frank is also a marine veteran, Pat an army veteran. He fought in the war in Vietnam and probably has a lot of interesting stories that he's never told, probably with good reason. Ron Lints worked for a long time at the Traverse City Iron Works and eventually went into the cement business. Frieda's husband is Roger Thompson, a local boy who ended up in the banking business. Being able to stay in the area and keep in pretty close contact with each other has been a great strength for all of us.

My aunts and uncles all had a pretty good sense of humor, as did my parents and grandparents. Many of the stories we heard as young kids came from relatives who sometimes told stories when they knew we were listening and sometimes when they thought we weren't. One of the first jokes I remember went, "Why does the ocean roar?" The other side came back with, "If you had crabs on your bottom, you'd roar, too."

To a ten-year-old, that was pretty humorous. I remember telling it to my teacher in school, Mrs. Pitcher, and she kind of giggled and got a red face. At that age I didn't understand why, but as I got older and into college and learned some things we didn't know in grade school, I understood a whole lot more.

Nowadays there's a lot of flap about sex education in the schools and whether or not it should be taught and how it should be taught and what exactly should be taught. I well remember my first sex education lesson. My teacher was Elsie Critchell, from Traverse City. About two-thirds of the way through the year, she had to take some time off, so the school board brought in Mrs. DeGraw as a substitute teacher. Mrs. DeGraw and her husband had been very good friends of the McManus family for many years and she was a well-accepted teacher in the community. Mrs. Critchell was a good teacher, too. In fact, all the grade school teachers I had were good.

One day I said to Mrs. DeGraw, "What's wrong with Mrs. Critchell? Why isn't she here teaching? Why does she have to take some time off?"

"She has to take some time off because she's going to have to have an operation," Mrs. DeGraw said. "She's got a tumor."

On the way home from school we always stopped at old Hattie Gehring's house, just north of the school. Hattie was also a very good friend of the family and she always made sure we got home safely. We'd stop at Hattie's to have a cookie and make a little conversation. I had the latest information, so as I was eating my cookie, I said, "Hattie, you know what's wrong with Mrs. Critchell?"

"What's wrong with Mrs. Critchell?" she replied.

"She's got a tumor."

Hattie started to giggle. "Yah. She's got a tumor all right. It's a squeaking tumor."

I tucked that little piece of information away and went on home. My mother was cooking supper, and I said, "At school today I asked Mrs. DeGraw what was wrong with Mrs. Critchell and Mrs. DeGraw told me she has a tumor. But then I stopped at Hattie's and told her about it and she said it was a squeaking tumor. Ma, what's a squeaking tumor?"

My mother had to explain that Mrs. Critchell was going to have a baby and that was the reason she had to take time off. Ma only told me as much as she cared to; she was rather skimpy on the details. I learned a whole lot more later on from my dad. In any event, my first sex education lesson had to do with a "squeaking tumor."

Like my dad, I attended K-7 at the Maple Grove School. My dad wasn't sure high school was absolutely necessary, but he went along with the fact that probably you should go, though he wanted me to attend public school rather than St. Francis. This was all because of an experience he had in the eighth grade.

Dad was one of the most street-smart men I ever met. After the seventh grade, his dad held him out for a year to help cut logs, so when he got ready to go into the eighth grade, he was a year older than the rest of the kids. He was bigger, and of course he'd been doing the work of a man by that time, and it was kind of embarrassing. As a young girl, his mother had attended St. Francis, the convent boarding school in Traverse City. She had boarded there and my great- grandfather had dropped her off along with produce from the farm to pay her tuition. She had a great love for the sisters, so she decided to send my dad to the Catholic school for his eighth grade year. In those days, you sent kids to school with a pen , pencil and crayon set. My dad also had a twelve-inch ruler in his packet. He had some of the equipment laid out on the desk one day when Julius Newberry was sitting behind him. Students were always seated alphabetically back then. Without asking, Julius reached up over Dad's shoulder and grabbed his ruler. That was a mistake on Newberry's part.

Dad was quick, and as Julius was raising his hand, he grabbed onto the ruler and between the two of them they snapped it in two. Dad stepped up from his desk and grabbed Julius by the shirt and decked him on the floor of the eighth grade classroom! I guess sister wasn't used to that kind of thing. She came down to straighten things out and told my dad they didn't allow fighting like that in the Catholic school.

Dad protested that Newberry had broken his ruler, but that didn't make any difference. Sister told him he had to apologize.

Dad said, "Apologize? Hell, he broke my ruler."

"You can't talk like that here," Sister said. "You'd better go see the priest."

The priest said even though he understood the situation, there was nothing he could do. If my dad wanted to stay in school, he'd have to apologize to appease the sister.

Dad decided it wasn't worth it and he quit, and that's why his education ended at the seventh grade as far as the formal part of it was concerned.

The peninsula was divided into seven school districts at one time: Old Mission, Ogdensburg, Mapleton, Bowers Harbor, Maple Grove, Stoney Beach, and McKinley. The Bowers Harbor School closed first and consolidated with Mapleton; by the time I was growing up, there were only six schools, all K-7.

Old Mission, Ogdensburg, and Mapleton were two-room schools, while Maple Grove, McKinley, and Stoney Beach were one-room schools. Each was under the direction of County School Superintendent George Eikey, but each school also had its own local school board consisting of a director, a moderator, and a treasurer. Grandpa McManus served as a moderator on the Maple Grove School Board for many, many years, including all the years I attended the school, which was located at the corner of Carroll and Center roads.

The year I entered, forty-two kids attended from the neighborhood. The district extended about a mile in each direction north and south and from East to West Bay. As you entered the school, you came through an entryway where the bell rope hung from the belfry. The bell was rung at 9:00, again at 10:45 when recess was over, at 1:00 when lunchtime was over, and at 2:45 when the afternoon recess ended. The only other time we were permitted to ring the bell, which never happened, was in case of a fire. Then we were to ring it steadily to bring help from the neighbors.

As you entered school from the door on the west end, the boys went to the right and the girls went to the left around the wall immediately in front of you in the entryway. On each of the corners was a shelf about two and one-half feet off the floor. That was where you placed your dinner pail or lunch bucket or paper sack, whatever you happened to have your lunch in, and periodically extra mittens and that type of thing. You could always tell who the rich kids were by the size of their lunch boxes. Rich kids had fancy lunch boxes; poor kids had sacks. They were even more well-to-do if they carried a thermos, but thermos bottles in lunch boxes weren't all that stable in those days. If you dropped your lunch or smashed it or used it to hit somebody, the thermoses tended to break, so they weren't all they were cracked up to be. Even so, those kids who had a thermos of hot chocolate were one notch above everyone else.

Lunches in those days usually consisted of sandwiches, either with store-bought or homemade bread. In the early days it was homemade, and generally the sandwiches were peanut butter or jam or peanut butter and jam together. Once in a while you might get lean beef with mustard. Usually mother sent along some cookies or something else, and there was usually an extra snack, which consisted of a half-sandwich or something else to eat at recess.

Our lunches were pretty good compared to what our parents and grandparents had. My dad never had to carry a lunch, because he lived close enough to go home at lunchtime, but my mother always talked about how sandwiches in earlier days were quite often lard on bread, which was something we never had to endure.

The so-called "hot lunch" came along a few years after we started school. Before this existed, we used to sometimes get grapefruit through a government commodity program; a dish of grapefruit sections at noon was quite a novelty.

We also had 4-H in our school. Mr. Ed Bopry, one of the parents, taught it and the boys all wanted to join because Bopry had a boat for succor spearing in the spring with a light on it. Anybody who was in 4-H got to go succor spearing in the bay with Mr. Bopry and his boat.

My first 4-H project was a window stop that all 4-H'ers made in handicraft. I also made my grandfather Fromholz a grain scoop out of a grapefruit can. I took the grapefruit can and cut it on a diagonal, which was quite a trick, and then cut out a dowel for a handle and screwed that to the grapefruit can cut in half on the diagonal. This was during World War II and I painted it red, white, and blue. I remember giving that to Grandpa Fromholz for a Christmas present. He kept it around for many, many years and gave it back to me probably forty years later.

Underneath the shelf for the lunch boxes was where you put the boots, and above the lunch boxes were hooks for coats and hats and scarves and the snow pants we wore in the wintertime. The recitation benches were up in front and pictures of George Washington and Abraham Lincoln hung on the wall, along with a clock on the front wall. Each class was required to come to the front and recite reading and spelling and arithmetic. We also had writing, and as we got into the upper grades, we diagrammed sentences on the blackboards that were in the front and around the walls of the school.

Each year at Christmas, we prepared for a Christmas program, a big event in the neighborhood. Everybody came to this program and each student was expected to perform either singly or in groups. As we got older, we also had box socials, as well as an annual spring picnic. A box social is a fundraiser where the girls prepare a box lunch or basket, well decorated, which is bid on by the boys, with the high bidder dining with the girl who prepared the basket. Sometimes you knew ahead of time who prepared which basket and sometimes you didn't.

The spring picnic was usually in June at the end of school. All the adults and children would gather, usually on a Sunday, for a potluck picnic. Games would be played before and after the meal and the school board would be elected for the coming year.

Essentially, the board's job was to hire the teacher, in our case, Mrs. Floyd (Lenora) Pitcher. She got fifty dollars a month for teaching school, but she didn't have to do the janitor work. They arranged for another person to do to this for fifteen dollars a month. In many cases the schoolteacher got thirty-five dollars and the janitor fifteen, but my grandfather felt Mrs. Pitcher was good enough that she should get all fifty dollars and not have to do the janitor work.

Most of the rural schoolteachers in our township were women. There were a few men like Les Jamieson, who taught at Mapleton as well as Drummond Island, but he was an anomaly. Mrs. Pitcher lived on State Street in Traverse City and on stormy days her husband, who worked at the railroad depot in the freight department, brought her out. There were only a few days when the roads didn't get snow-plowed enough for her to get out to school.

The school grounds were big enough to have a ball diamond, so we played softball when we didn't have snow. We used the old system of choosing sides in which you grasped the bat and each side went hand over hand, with whoever reached the top of the bat (no eagle claws allowed) getting to decide who batted first. I usually played left field, and boys and girls played together. We had to include everybody in order to have enough players.

In the wintertime we built forts and had snowball fights and went sledding on a small incline on the back of the playground. When the teacher wasn't looking, we sometimes played Eenie I Over, where you throw the ball over the schoolhouse roof and run around to tag the person who catches it.

Our school didn't have a heated toilet. We did have a furnace in the basement of the school, but the boys' and girls' toilets were in an unheated room that was added on to the building. It was kind of a special arrangement to keep the toilets from freezing in the winter. Still, we were lucky not to have outside toilets like we had at home or like some of the schools.

I took part in my first private property discussion in grade school. We needed some bases to play softball, so one of the older boys brought four gunnysacks to school one day along with a shovel. We were going to fill the sacks with dirt and use them for bases. The next-door neighbor had a cherry orchard just on the other side of the schoolyard fence. The ground was worked up so it was nice and loose and easy to shovel, whereas the playground was mostly sod, so some of the boys went over and scooped up some shovels of earth to fill the four bags.

Then they brought them back and placed them at first, second, third, and home bases.

A day or two later, the owner of the property came over to talk to the teacher. He said somebody had been in his orchard and taken some dirt without permission and he wanted it back. I remember the teacher instructing us to take the bags back and refill the holes where we'd gotten the dirt. People had a great respect for private property in those days, and I expect that's carried along with me ever since.

When I was in the fifth grade, we had a township spelling bee. All six of the operating schools in the township picked their local winner and sent him or her to the town hall for the final spelldown. I won that year, and for a prize I received a Winston Dictionary with a green cover. I recall using that dictionary all the way through high school and into college.

By the time I finished seventh grade at Maple Grove, attendance at the school was down to thirty-five. The school operated for some time after that, but eventually it consolidated with the rest of the peninsula schools and then eventually was annexed to Traverse City.

Mrs. Pitcher was an excellent teacher. She brought forth a great number of students who successfully went into various occupations. She had a lot of common sense. I remember on Sunday, December 7, 1941, the Japanese bombed Pearl Harbor. We came to school on Monday and Mrs. Pitcher brought out a radio. We had quite a discussion about the war and so on and one of the neighbor boys wanted to know whether or not the Germans were black. We had a German family in the neighborhood and they were all very, very blond. Mrs. Pitcher said to the neighbor boy, "Take a look at Maxine there. Is she black? You know she's German." I don't expect he ever forgot that.

Mrs. Pitcher not only had to instruct us, discipline us, and teach us the ways of the world, she also had to put up with a lot of different things not particularly related to education. One of them was head lice. We didn't have pesticides to control them like we have today, and it's just something that happened in rural schools. In those days, you were instructed to go home and rinse your hair with kerosene. That would get the lice all right, but then you still had the nits, the little eggs that had to be kerosened once or twice more or picked off by your mother.

We also had a couple of girls who wet their pants until about the fourth grade before they quit. That was kind of a mess. We also had the usual episodes of measles and mumps and chicken pox and all those types of things.

We never did have a hot lunch program that I recall in the Maple Grove School, but I did attend McKinley School one year and that year they'd already instituted hot lunch. We had a stove there and the students and the teacher would cook the lunch, along with some government surplus foods we got. We were able to have one hot dish along with the sandwiches or whatever else we'd brought from home.

The instruction we got in those days carried us through life very well. We were given a good basic understanding of the English language. We also understood addition, subtraction, multiplication, division, spelling, and pronunciation, and we were given instruction in several other subjects. The old system of the rural school, with seven or eight grades in one room with recitation, probably was one of the most innovative systems of education in the world. It basically took care of a situation that's a real problem today. Back then, slow learners heard a repetition of each lesson year after year, while the fast learners were always able to hear the recitation of the grades ahead of them. The fast ones could move faster and the slow ones could catch up, a much better system of learning than the segmented system we have now.

The classes were small when I started school. Joyce Miller and I were two kindergartners, while Bernice Buchan was a grade ahead of us. Eventually Mrs. Pitcher put the three of us together, which caused Joyce and me to skip the third grade and go directly into fourth.

Today's maps of the peninsula show the villages of Old Mission and Mapleton, but the village called Archie is missing from the map. Archie was located at the intersection of Gray Road and M-37. There was a post office there at one time, and Grandma McManus, who was born a Carroll, told me she attended school there before the Maple Grove School was built. The recreational spot known as Archie Park is still there, but the old hall where I played volleyball in the wintertime is gone. Nonetheless, in the 1930s, we were always considered to be from Archie rather than from Mapleton or Old Mission. The Archie Farm Bureau group and the Archie Women's Club were both in existence in my lifetime, and my father was a ballplayer on the Archie baseball team, coached by my great-uncle Andy Carroll.

I only remember one real problem in our school, when one of the boys bit Mrs. Pitcher on the arm one day. She had bent down to correct something he was doing at his desk, and when she put her hand out, he reached up and bit her. That caused quite a lot of consternation in the neighborhood. My grandfather and the rest of the school board had a little meeting with the boy's parents. I don't know exactly what they told him, but he never bit the teacher again and things went along all right after that.

We used to walk a mile to school, which people laugh about today. We usually tried to get there before school began so we could play ball or throw snowballs or something with the other kids. Recess was at 10:30 for fifteen minutes, and then we had an hour off for dinner. We were back in class at 1:00, afternoon recess was at 2:30 for fifteen minutes, and we were done for the day at 4:00. Attendance was pretty regular.

Vaccinations took place at the school and the county health nurse, Miss Farr, came periodically to check us for different things. We never had any serious health issues. All in all, students who went to that school moved up in life and many of them have done pretty well given the small beginning they had.

My closest pal all through life, my cousin John (Jack) Gallagher, lived long enough to see me elected to the Senate in 1990. He passed on from cancer shortly after that, cancer that I can't help but believe was probably related to the fact that he served in the Korean conflict. John was the son of my Aunt Marjorie McManus Gallagher and her husband Cecil Gallagher. The Gallaghers lived on a farm west of Traverse City, a big dairy farm with a few cherries to boot. In the days we were growing up, there were ten Gallagher kids and seven of us McManus kids. We got together regularly, so John and I became fast friends and pals as well as cousins over the years.

We were born 364 days apart. He was born on December 13 of 1929 and I was born on December 12 of 1930, but we were in the same grade in school and attended grades 8-12 at St. Francis together. John's grandfather, old John Gallagher, came to the United States from Ireland in the late 1800s and arrived in the Traverse City area about 1890. He married a lady who had been married before to a man by the name of Smith, so the Gallaghers have several half cousins from the Smith husband. One of those, Nellie, married an Ankerson. All Nelly's children are related to the Gallaghers, so I suppose that makes them shirttail relatives of ours.

Old John Gallagher had several children: Blanche Wurm, Alice Kilmartin, Cecil, Leo, and I don't know; there may have been others from the Gallagher side. He also had a brother who ended up in the Tupperware business. Traverse City originally had the Oval Wood Dish Factory and made dishes out of wood; that firm eventually moved to Tupper Lake, New York, Or so I am told.

Young John grew up on a farm partly located in Garfield Township and partly in Long Lake Township, where his dad had a sizeable dairy herd of black and white Holsteins. They did have some cherries, because Aunt Marjorie was from a cherry farm on the peninsula and she insisted on having cherries.

John was the oldest of the ten children and carried out many responsibilities on the farm from the time he was a young boy. He was a good, husky, barrel-chested, black-haired Irishman full of fun and very knowledgeable about many things I needed to know about that I didn't get told out on the peninsula. So John and I got along royally and did many things in life together. In addition to Douglas Gallagher, John had two other brothers, Jim and Babe (Gary), and six sisters, Betty, Margaret (also called "Sister"), Colleen, Dorothy, Mary, and Linda. Those cousins of mine have been very close to me over the years and have given me a lot of help.

John married Bernadine Korson from Gill's Pier and had seven children, three boys (John Jr., Martin, and Joe) and four girls (Maria, Debbie, Jeannie, and Margaret). John also had a sizeable cherry farm in the Lincoln Road area at the base of Leelanau County and he and I worked very closely back in 1972 along with Terry Morrison from Cherry Growers and others in the reorganization of that company. At that point, it was slated to go out of business and the cherry farmers in northern Michigan would have lost a considerable market for their fruit. We worked together to reorganize the cooperative and put it back in business. Since then, it has returned many millions of dollars to fruit growers, not only in northern Michigan but also to farmers in central and southern Michigan who are part of the 164 members of that cooperative.

John was also active on the Production Credit Association board and in the Farmers Mutual Insurance Company. He played a very active role in agricultural business in northwestern Michigan and was sorely missed when he passed on, not only by his family but by many other people in the Grand Traverse region.

John came in from Lone Tree School out at the west side of town after the sixth grade and attended seventh grade at St. Francis. Some of the city kids were giving him a hard time and I had good grades, so he wanted me to come in to St. Francis with him and show them city kids up.

I wanted to go to St. Francis because he went there. My mother didn't say much one way or another, but my dad had didn't want me to do it, so I went up and talked to Grandma McManus. As I said earlier, she thought a lot of that school and wanted as many of her grandkids to attend as possible. Grandma said, "If you want to go to St. Francis, it's to St. Francis you'll go. If your father has a problem with that, you tell him to come see me."

The next time the subject came up, I said I was going to go to St. Francis with John Gallagher. I added, "I was up talkin' to Grandma Mack, and Grandma said if anybody had a problem with that they could come talk to her about it."

Well, we never heard any more about it. I went to St. Francis and eventually graduated from high school there, along with John Gallagher. Oh, about the two people I was supposed to show up, one of them ended up the valedictorian and the other the historian. I was the salutatorian, so I was able to help take care of John's problem.

I was only the second McManus grandchild to attend college. The first was my cousin Vivian from Kingsley. At that time, you had to have a reference to go to Michigan State and I didn't know any Michigan Staters, so I got cousin Vivian to sign my papers and she got a girl-friend of hers, a person I never met, to be the second signer.

The reason I went to Michigan State had to do with scholar-ships. The bishop offered one scholarship in the diocese to attend St. Thomas Aquinas College in Grand Rapids for all the Catholic schools at the time, and I had taken the test and won it. At the same time, in the twelfth grade, while taking physics over at the public high school, I noticed that two senatorial scholarships were being offered at Michigan State College. The teacher handling the applications helped me fill out the forms and I sent in my credits and grades. Eventually, I got a letter saying I had been awarded a senatorial scholarship to attend Michigan State College.

I didn't know what to do. I had the bishop's scholarship to St. Thomas Aquinas College and the senatorial scholarship to Michigan State, so one morning I went to the principal at St. Francis and told her I had a problem.

Sister Austin said, "Young man, what's the problem?"

"I've got these two scholarships," I answered, "one to Thomas Aquinas and one to Michigan State, and I don't know which one to take."

"Which one pays the most money?" she asked.

"The one to Michigan State. It's four years' tuition."

She looked straight at me and said, "If I were you, that's the one I'd go for."

That solved that problem. I am probably the only senator in Michigan who attended college on one of those senatorial scholarships!

As I said, I transferred from the Maple Grove School to St. Francis in Traverse City in the eighth grade. We had fifty-two kids in the eighth grade and the teacher was Sister Kathleen Bannon. We were bussed in, and each morning the bus came early enough, we attended mass before we went to school. Each grade sat as a group with a nun behind them. The sisters all had a frog, a little metal clicker they used to get everyone to stand up and sit down. After mass, we attended classes, and when school started everyone had to be in their seats. When the bell rang, we immediately stood for prayers and after prayers we had to sit down in absolute silence. There was no monkeying around.

Sister conducted the lessons much the same as Mrs. Pitcher had. One thing that was a little different was the priest came over each marking period and passed out the report cards to the students. One by one, you had to go to the front of the room and he'd read over the marks and tell you whether you were doing as well as he thought you should be. That would probably be unheard of today, but nobody thought too much of it in those days. I was a very good student, getting mostly all A's, so it didn't bother me, but it probably bothered some of the kids.

I remember one incident from those days. The assistant pastor at St. Francis was Father Walzer, a displaced person from Germany who had fled the Nazis in World War II by getting on his bicycle one afternoon and riding into Switzerland. He was from southern Germany and had been preaching against the Nazi regime. On his final Sunday in church, as he preached his sermon, he saw six Nazi agents in the front row taking notes. He knew his time was up, so he got on his bicycle and rode to Switzerland. When he got to the border, the German guards wouldn't let him through. He punched the guard and had teeth marks in his fist for several days after. The Swiss guards let him cross, and from there he flew to Brazil and then came into the United States and ultimately ended up at St. Francis. Somehow he got acquainted with my folks, and every once in a while he stopped at the farm and my mother would get out the liverwurst and rye bread and my dad would get out a bottle of beer and they'd make real conversation about Germany and what was going on over there. I suppose meeting him is one of the things that interested me in European travel and what was going on in the rest of the world.

One other experience interested me in foreign countries. A Finnish lady by the name of Lydia Kotalanian came to our school when I was still schooling on the peninsula and presented a PTA program one night on Lapland. She brought some clothing and different things from that country that I found fascinating.

In the eighth grade at St. Francis, Father Walzer used to come over and talk religion once in a while. One day a question was asked that nobody could answer but me, so I raised my hand and he had me stand up and recite the answer. Then he said to the rest of the class, "You see, McManus here comes from out on the peninsula. He lives on those high hills out there where the wind blows the cobwebs out of his brains." He was chastising the rest of them for not having studied the lesson. I don't know whatever happened to him, but he was a very interesting character, another one of those people who added to my interests in life.

High school, which included grades nine through twelve, was upstairs in the old St. Francis School. There were twenty-five in my grade, twelve boys and thirteen girls. The other three grades were about the same. I took two years of Latin and of course English and algebra and geometry and trigonometry and chemistry and government and religion and all the various college prep courses. Our school didn't have enough students interested in physics to teach it, so in our senior year seven of us walked over to the public high school, located at that time between Seventh and Eighth streets. Mr. Bernie Kirk was our teacher. From there we caught the bus home. Mary Zoulek, one of my fellow students, was interested in art and she went over with us at the same time. Bud Johnson was in wood shop and he too took several classes at the public school. These various students and the two schools worked together very closely.

The nuns were excellent teachers. They had degrees from several universities, several of them from Notre Dame. They had taught at various schools throughout northern Michigan as well as in their mission in New Mexico, so they had experience from several parts of the country.

I graduated from St. Francis as salutatorian. Phyllis Kunky beat me out for valedictorian by a fraction of a point. She ended up a nurse. Bob Harmon was the historian of our class and he ended up an attorney in Chicago. I went from a high school graduating class of twenty-five to Michigan State College, which in the fall of 1948 had 14,000 students. This was a huge change.

Sister Austin, my high school principal all the way through, was also my mathematics teacher, and Sister Rose Kathleen Carroll was our English teacher. She taught us Shakespeare and helped us put on *The Merchant of Venice*. She was also a graduate of Notre Dame and very versed in Shakespearian literature. Sister Andrea taught chemistry, Sister Dorothea was the homeroom teacher, Sister Agnes Therese taught Latin, Sister Lorraine was our eleventh grade homeroom teacher, Sister Rose Catherine taught government, and I may have left out one or two. Our band instructor was Mr. Dykie, followed by Miss Levine. Sister Stephana was my first piano teacher, followed by Sister Matilda.

When I first got to Michigan State, I lived in a Quonset hut for a few weeks. MSC had done a great job with the veterans after World War II, putting up a lot of temporary housing to take care of the influx of soldiers coming back from the war to get an education. John Hannah, the president of the college, was a tremendous educator who had the foresight to get the housing in and make education available to those returning veterans. Eventually I got into the old Wells Hall dormitory with Doug Steiger and Dick Kratochvil from Traverse City. I lived there for a year before I got married.

President John Hannah put on a dinner each term for students who had made all A's; he usually had between sixty-two and sixty-five students out of the 14,000. I attended several of these dinners. After we were married, Clara went with me. We'd have dinner in the Union Building and then sit around the table while Hannah asked each of us where we were from. We came from schools all over Michigan, big and small, and Hannah always said, "It doesn't make any difference whether you come from a big or a small school, a big town or a small town. When you come to Michigan State College and if you apply yourself and study hard, you can become a success."

I've thought about that many times, how the students from the big and small schools were about equally successful when they got to college. All these people, as well as Mrs. Pitcher, Mrs. Critchell, Mrs. DeGraw, and the various professors at Michigan State, had a great and positive influence on my life.

People like to hear the story of how I met my wife, Clara. I always tell them I was driving my dad's '35 Chevrolet ton and a half truck one day down Secor Road between Silver Lake and Long Lake when I saw this gal in a pasture dressed in a bikini. A cow was tied to a post and she was milking the cow. I'd never seen anything like that on the peninsula, so I brought the truck to a screeching halt and got out and asked if she'd like to go to the fair. (It was Northwestern Michigan Fair week.) She said she would, and if I'd finish milking the cow, she'd go get ready. She handed me the pail and I sat down and finished milking the cow while she went to the house to get dressed. I usually add that I've been working for her ever since!

That is a true story, except that I did know Clara a little bit before that. The first time I ever met her was on the school bus back in about the ninth grade, when she went home one night with Gloria Gore, a cousin of mine on the peninsula. She and Gloria were school chums at Traverse City Public School. I think we got into an argument over which school taught Latin better, St. Francis or the public school. She didn't make much of an impression on me then, but in the eleventh grade, she switched over to St. Francis and that was a little unusual. Usually kids either started in grade school or at least started at the ninth grade level at the high school. But her mother, Ellen Courtade, had been a graduate of St. Francis. In fact, she was the valedictorian of the class of 1923.

Right away, Clara was elected the president of the junior class. We only had twenty-five students, but it was still an honor, and she was nominated by several students she'd gotten to know in the first few days of classes. The president of the junior class had the responsibility of putting on the senior prom in the spring of the junior year up at the old country club. As president of the class, she needed a date to take her to the dance and thats where I came in ,

I wasn't much of a dancer, but I got up my nerve and asked if I could take her to the prom. She allowed as how I could, so I borrowed a jacket from Uncle Carl McManus and bought myself a pair of white buck saddle shoes and her mother made her a dress and off we went. We dated a little bit after that, but in the summer she got busy working in the Long Lake area and I was busy on the peninsula, so we didn't really get going again until about Christmas of our senior year. At that time, I asked if she'd go with me to midnight mass.

The rest of that winter, our dates pretty much consisted of going to the grange dances in Grawn, Michigan, where all the young people from her neighborhood went to square dance, fox trot, and so on. She was a very good dancer, and though I had to learn bit by bit, we got along. I was president of the class our twelfth grade year, and we courted some the summer between our senior year and college, then continued dating when I went to Michigan State College after high school and she went to St. Lawrence nurse's training in Lansing.

I came home to farm the summer after the first year of college while she stayed in Lansing in her nurse's training. That didn't work out very well. After a few weeks, I called her up and asked her to think about getting married, which we did in August before we went back to college that fall.

Clara was a very interesting person to me, to say the least. Many of the virtues I was looking for in a future wife were prominent in her personality. She had a good sense of humor, was quite a serious person, and carried herself well in all kinds of situations. I don't know what love is, but that's what struck me, and we ended up getting married and carrying out our life's plan of raising a large family of nine and also having a sizeable cherry orchard.

Lots of things happened in between, but it all worked out in the end. It's amazing that if you set your goals rather high in the beginning and find the right person to help you, things seem to work out. Clara worked at the hospital for a year after we were married, helping me through college, and she also worked some at the Kellogg Center during her college days. In Traverse City, she worked at Bellaws Restaurant in the summertime along with my sister. She even picked enough cherries to buy my suit for our wedding, so we've worked it out over the years.

Her dad gave her mother $250 to put on our wedding, which was what he planned to do for all four of his daughters. Her mother, a rather shrewd person, decided we needed the $250 so she said if I could arrange for our wedding dance and also pay the band, she'd take care of the rest of it and we could have the money.

We had a brunch on our wedding day of roast chicken and mashed potatoes, practically a full course meal, put on by all her friends. We had a dance that night at the Garfield Town Hall. Dad told me to go with him to buy the drinks for the dance. Ray Courtade had a distributorship for beer and wine in the Traverse City area, and Dad told me to tell Ray I was Frieda Fromholz' son and that I was getting married and I wanted to buy some beer and wine for the dance. I did as he said and Ray gave me a discount. Dad told me afterwards that my mother had dated Ray Courtade in the early days and she knew him pretty well.

After our wedding, Clara went to work at St. Lawrence Hospital as a nurses' aide helping to "PHT" (Push Hubby Through), which was a common term at the time. Many of the wives worked and helped their husbands get a college education. We lived in a small trailer park north of campus on M-78 where we rented a spot for fifteen dollars a month.

We carried on a full year that way. The next spring, we came north and farmed through the summer. We sold our fruit at the Eastern Farmers Market that fall in Detroit and didn't go back to college until

January. As I said earlier, I graduated at the end of thirteen terms with a master's degree and a 3.94 average out of a possible 4. All in all, I got one C in college, in a one-credit badminton course. I never won a game all season! I ended up with a combination of horticulture as my major and agricultural economics as my minor, which I felt was a good combination for anyone going into my line of business. Dr. Al Kenworthy was my major professor in horticulture.

After the children started to come along, Clara was only able to work part-time. I would come back to married housing and study and she would work some at the Kellogg Center as a waitress. When we graduated from college, we didn't owe anybody any money and we had three kids paid for. In those days, hospitalization costs were a little different. For our oldest daughter, Lisa, the doctor bill was twenty-five dollars and the hospital bill was thirty-two dollars, which we paid in cash. When Molly was born, the doctor was up to something like thirty-five dollars and the hospital was about forty-five dollars, which we paid in cash. The first two were born in Traverse City, but Peggy was born in Lansing. She was baptized there too, at St. Thomas Catholic Church. There the doctor bill was seventy-five dollars and the hospital bill was one hundred dollars. So with the first three girls, we didn't have any such thing as hospital insurance or Blue Cross; we paid in cash. Later on we got insurance and the rest of the kids were covered by that policy.

I don't expect many people in the world have been gravediggers, or the sexton of a cemetery, but when I graduated from college in 1953 and Clara and I and our young daughters moved back to the peninsula, I was asked to be the sexton of the Catholic cemetery at St. Joseph and take care of the grave digging. In those days, you were paid fifteen dollars for digging a grave. That wasn't too bad on the west end of the cemetery, back where the ground is sandy, but on the east half of the cemetery, where the ground is pretty much hard clay, you earned your fifteen dollars. Most people talk about being buried six feet under, but the truth is, very few people are buried at that depth. Generally speaking, about four and one-half feet is as far as the holes go.

When I first became sexton, there wasn't any cribbing for the graves. You could dig a hole on clay ground that was good and solid, but when you got into the sandier area, the sides had a tendency to cave in. We were digging a grave one time next to where my Aunt Lizzie was buried and I thought for sure she was going to come slidin' over into the hole. In addition, the pall bearers always stood alongside the caskets when they were lowered, and it could be embarrassing if they slid into the hole because of the caving in. I talked to the good father, Father Farrell, and told him we really ought to have some cribbing, so the church committee got busy and bought some 2 by 12's and after that we had cribbing in the sandy part of the cemetery.

There's a lot of history in the cemetery, which straddles the fence between the Hoffman farm and what was originally the Lawrence Carroll farm. If you go back through the records, you'll find many of the old families on the peninsula, several generations of them, are buried there. The old settlers were buried in the front row at the east side, and for a while the generations progressively worked their way back. My great-grandfather Edward Carroll and his wife are buried there and my great-grandfather Thomas Arthur McManus and his wife Mary should be, but as I covered earlier, they're buried in unmarked graves at the Ogdensburg cemetery. My grandparents Arthur Thomas and Eliza Jane are buried in the front end of the north side in what were to be the greatgrandparents graves and my parents are behind them. Clara and I have a lot over on the south side of the cemetery, about halfway back.

When I moved out to the Garfield Road residence in 1956, I was happy to pass the sexton responsibility onto the next person. Keeping the records wasn't too bad, but digging the graves, especially in the wintertime, was a difficult situation for the money that was involved.

Things were different then in other ways, too. When I first got out of college and went back to the peninsula, I was elected Justice of the Peace for a year or two. I only had one case. A dog had killed a bunch of chickens, and under the dog license fees, this entitled the farmer to compensation. The killing had occurred at Ted Ayres' place and I had to go down and make a determination so Ted could collect his compensation. Before I went, I read over the Justice of the Peace book for Peninsula Township. There were only three or four cases in the whole history of the township, but one was very interesting. I don't know where that book is now, but I hope someone has kept it, as I returned it when my term was up.

The Justice wrote out in longhand how the constable had brought the prisoner before him, the prisoner having been involved in a domestic violence case. The justice decided to remand the prisoner to the county prison, but it was a cold and stormy night and a long ways to Traverse City to where the prison was located, so rather than carry out the sentence and go to town, the Justice decided to fine the defendant three dollars. On the next line, it says, "Whereas the defendant didn't have the $3 to pay, he, the Justice, decided to loan him the $3 in order to get the case solved." There's a notation at the bottom of the page, written about twenty years later, in which the justice writes, "As of this time, the loan has not been repaid." I guess there's some charity in the world after all!

About the time I got out of college and came home, there was a lot of talk about consolidating and annexing the peninsula schools to Traverse City. The rural grade schools had always operated independently through the seventh grade, then sent their children into Traverse City for high school. Some rural districts annexed to Traverse City early on, but for a long time most tried to avoid that, though later they went though a series of consolidations.

My dad was an early advocate of consolidation of the six peninsula school districts into one school district on the peninsula. He spent two or three winters on a committee, along with Ellis Wunsch and Becky Tompkins and others, trying to get the various districts to do this. It was quite an effort. Some of the people in the McKinley district wanted to annex directly to Traverse City and there were other lines of thought as to what should be done as well. Dad knew the various districts probably would annex to Traverse City sooner or later, but if he could get the districts on the peninsula to consolidate into one district and build a school, the little kids from Old Mission who lived twenty miles north of Traverse City wouldn't have to travel that long distance on the bus every day to and from town; they could have their own permanent grade school right out there in the township. Eventually all six districts voted to consolidate into the Old Mission Peninsula School.

During that discussion, a big brouhaha developed on where the building should be. Various locations were studied, and finally the back end of the Hoffman farm and part of the Raymond Carroll farm next door was chosen, a beautiful site the Hoffmans had never planted to cherries. There was a hayfield up there when I was a kid; it was a great site overlooking Bowers Harbor and a grand place for a school. Dad was pretty adamant that the school go on that spot. Others wanted it down where the Bowers Harbor ballpark is now. There was some land north of that, between the road that runs past the ballpark at Bowers Harbor and the road running to Peninsula Fruit Exchange. That land could have been bought a little cheaper, for five hundred dollars or so an acre rather than a thousand an acre, but the advocates of the better site on the hill prevailed and eventually the school was built where it sits today.

One of the other interesting questions at the time was how deep they were going to have to drill for water. Because the peninsula was laid down by glaciers, the water patterns are quite varied. When we first moved to our home farm, for instance, the well was fifty feet deep. It was a dug well, but you could only get one barrel of water at a time and you had to wait after getting that one barrel until the well filled up again so you could get another. When we eventually got around to drilling something better than that, we drilled a six-inch well and had to go down 220 feet. Most drilled wells on the peninsula were at that 200-foot level, and everybody was worried about how deep they were going to have to go at the school because it was on a hill.

Bids were accepted and a firm from Clare got the bid, figuring they'd probably have to go 250 to 300 feet. They started drilling one morning and my dad went up about noon to ask how they were coming. They said it was a bad situation: they'd bid the job figuring they'd have to go to great depths, but they'd hit water at ninety feet, and at noon, they already had water! It was going to be a money-losing proposition, since they'd brought their rig clear from Clare.

For several years the school had water from that ninety-foot well, which was a big surprise to everyone. I understand now they've had to drill deeper than that, but you never know on the peninsula at what depth you're going to hit a vein of water.

Art Glidden, the county agricultural agent in Grand Traverse County, was following my activities pretty closely. When I got out of college, I was immediately elected by the farmers onto the Agricultural Stabilization Committee and the Grand Traverse County Cherry Producers Association. I was also tied into the local Farm Bureau.

In the meantime, Michigan State Extension had been hoping to hire an extension marketing agent for the area. The fruit associations had been working to get that position going, and eventually some funding came through from Washington. In the spring of 1956, I was offered that job.

This was kind of traumatic, because my parents expected me to stay on the farm, even though I had four other brothers, but I finally made up my mind that if extension would pay me twice what I was making farming, I'd do it. When they asked me, I told them, "If you'll pay me $6,000 a year, you've got yourself a man." They couldn't wait to get the papers out. I found out later they had been prepared to pay me $6,500!

I didn't go to work for extension July 1 when they wanted me to, because my dad had quite a fit over the whole situation and wanted me to help him sell fruit that fall at the Eastern Farmers Market in Detroit, so I delayed my start date until November 1 of 1956.

At the time I went to work for extension, the staff in the basement of the post office in Traverse City included Art Glidden, Clarence Mullett, Edna (Deo) Alsup, Andy Olson, and Ruth Hunsberger. All of them had many years of experience in extension and they each, in one way or another, gave me a great deal of help and advice on how to handle an extension appointment. My work included doing radio and other types of media work, farm visits, and transferring information from the research done at MSU in the agricultural experiment station to people in the Grand Traverse region.

I would be remiss if I did not relate the story of how the Northwest Michigan Horticultural Research Station was initiated and developed. Toward the end of my extension career, the dean of agriculture at Michigan State University, Jim Anderson, by training an agricultural engineer and new on the job, came up to visit me to observe mechanical cherry harvesters in action. During our tour of orchards, we stopped at Bob Underwood's farm market on McKinley Road. Bob brought up the subject of a research station for our area, something growers in the area had long discussed. In essence, the dean said, "Why don't you build one?" Bob jumped on it and we proceeded to involve Pete Morrison, who involved many others as the movement spread. We raised $500,000 from the agricultural community and purchased the land and built the building that originally comprised the station. The Gregory boys, Bob and Don, were helpful in securing the site and Dr. Charles Kesner, our horticulture agent, played a major part in developing it. This was a major accomplishment for the cherry industry in northwest Michigan as well as other areas of the U.S. I was proud to be part of it.

When I went to work for extension, we paid my dad and brothers to operate our farm for a while in conjunction with their activities, but later on, as our kids got old enough, they planted trees and picked rocks and sprayed. For a while we hired migrant workers to pick cherries, but eventually we went to machines. At the same time, we were able to carry on a twenty-five-year career with the extension service,

Vice President George H. W. Bush, Governor Bill Milliken, and me on a hay wagon at the dedication of the Northwest Michigan Horticultural Research Station

which gave us an income to cover the cost it takes to raise a family while you're going along. Nonetheless, things got pretty touchy in the early '60s, when the price of cherries went to a nickel a pound and the price of cattle dropped in one year from forty-two cents to twenty-three cents.

After I began paying him back, my dad set out some young orchards trying to get my brothers started. He started my brother Frank over on Hartman Road and eventually my brother Art on Garfield and later on Mike and Pat, but he was getting into problems with the Production Credit Association (PCA), his financing source. I remember the bank of St. Paul sending a regional representative over to see him to tell him he had to make some changes in the way he farmed.

I remember Dad telling me, "Now you set down and watch this meeting, because one thing you never do is let the banker run your farm." He said, "If the price of potatoes is up this year, they want you to plant potatoes. And if you plant potatoes, then everybody else is plantin' potatoes and the price will be down when you get ready to sell. So then the next year they won't want you to grow potatoes cause the price is down, so you don't plant the potatoes and then nobody plants, so the price goes up, so when the price is up you haven't got any potatoes and you're never goin to win under that situation."

I can remember the young banker, a redheaded fellow. Of course he had all the answers, and with his white shirt and necktie on, he told my dad what he ought to do. My dad finally told him, "If you want to run this farm, you don't belong in an office in St. Paul, Minnesota. You belong right here. Other than that, you can pack your bags and go back over there and we'll run it."

In the end, Dad wanted the money he had coming from me on the land contract in order to pay against short-term borrowings he had with the PCA. I wasn't obligated to pay it under the terms of our land contract, but Dad needed the money. The PCA said they would loan the money to me, then I could give it to Dad, who in turn could pay off his debt.

I agreed to it, but the PCA interest rate was a little more than what Dad was charging me on the contract so I demanded a discount for whatever it was, I suppose five hundred dollars or something. Dad was pretty upset about it. He couldn't understand why I shouldn't pay the full principle, even if I had to pay another percent interest, rather than pay at the discount. Finally Production Credit told him it was fair enough, so he went along with the deal.

But I didn't want to pay the PCA's interest; I wanted to refinance the whole thing with the Federal Land Bank, which is supposed to be the long-term financing for farmers. I hoped to put the house and farm together and get a long-term loan for about five percent. Production Credit was willing to help me do that if it was possible, so we called on a land bank officer to make out a loan application. In the meantime, I went to local banks to try to borrow what I needed, $30,000, and the State Bank turned me down. The National Bank did approve a loan for me, but they wanted monthly payments on the interest in place of an annual payment of interest and principal. They also had to have something like six and one-half percent interest.

I took that and paid Production Credit off, but I still pursued the land bank because they had an annual payment system and also a lower rate. Howard Bedell, their loan officer for our area, came down from Bellaire to fill out the paperwork for that application. We sat down at a table and he asked me what the farm was worth on the inventory sheet and I told him and he subtracted a little bit. Then he asked me what the house was worth and I told him and he subtracted a little more. The upshot of it was, we got turned down, but Leonard Christenson, manager of our local PCA, took the evidence up to the district offices of the land bank in St. Paul on his next trip and laid it out in front of the board of directors of the Farm Credit System and they came through. They told old Bedell to loan one-half million dollars in the next six months or they didn't need him around and they'd close up his office. (The PCA, Federal Land Bank, and Bank for Cooperatives were all part of the Farm Credit System in those days.)

Bedell called me up and wanted to know if I still wanted that $30,000. I did, so he came down and we sat in exactly the same chairs at the same table and filled out the same set of inventory papers. Eventually we learned that our $30,000 loan had been approved, but we'd have to buy $1,500 worth of stock in the land bank. That kind of got to me, and I went to Leonard Christenson and asked him what I should do. He said, "Well, you've played it this far; why don't you play it the rest of the way?"

I wrote them back and told them I was sorry, but if their stock was any good I thought they ought to loan me the $30,000 plus the $1,500 for the stock.

I got a letter back in a little while that said, "We have reevaluated your situation. We find you are eligible for a $32,000 loan, $30,000 to pay off National Bank, $1,600 for stock, and $400 for extraneous purposes."

That gave me a long-term twenty-year loan at a lower rate of interest and that was the basis of the beginnings of our farming operation. Anything we have accumulated, we have accumulated from there. We started out with exactly nothing on the farm and only $250 to buy a house and build our property and our farm business from that point forward.

Thankfully, the extension service work provided Clara and me with a steady income to raise the nine children we were blessed with. We also had one child, Rosemary, who was stillborn; she's buried in the cemetery at St. Joseph's in Mapleton. Of the nine who lived, we had three sons. George III married Lori Piggot and is a farmer in the Benton Harbor area. Her dad had a sizeable farm raising , strawberries, cucumbers, and tomatoes. Lori's parents had six girls and no boys and the other sons-in-laws were not particularly interested in farming, so Mr. Piggott asked George to go into farming with him. It's a good farm, well located, close to the Benton Harbor market with available supplies of land and irrigation equipment. George raises a sizeable amount of the vegetable crops so he has a sizeable labor force for picking and packing. He and Lori have four children, Amy Rose, Erin, Emily, and George IV.

John, our second son, is farming the cherry farm at Traverse City. He's married to the former Michelle Rodebaugh. The Rodebaughs are from Traverse City and her mother was a Petrosky, an old family in the area. Clara and I went to school with Michelle's aunt, Barbara Petrosky, who married a fellow classmate of mine from the peninsula, Jack Kelly. John and Michelle have three children, John Ryan, Genevieve, and Jacob.

Matthew, our youngest son, married Lisa Wills, Phil and Rita Wills' oldest daughter. The Wills came into the Traverse City area from

Houghton Lake and Lisa attended St. Francis School, where she and Matt met. They have a son, Matthew.

Our girls begin with Eliza Jane, who's named after Grandmother McManus, one of the prominent figures in my life. We call her Lisa, at her direction. She is a graduate of Michigan State University in interior design with a year of training at Loyola University in Rome, Italy, in art and architecture. She was employed in the furniture business in Grand Rapids. She's married to Stu Saints, a local businessman in Traverse City. They have two adopted daughters from China, Sarah and Hannah, who are very active young ladies, and a son Carlos from Guatemala, a very active young lad.

Our second daughter is Molly Sue. Molly married Nicholas Agostinelli, whose family were construction people in Midland. Nick's mother is Hungarian and his father is from the southern part of Italy, not far from the town of Bari on the Adriatic Sea. Clara and I have visited some of Nick's cousins who are still in that village. Nick came up to Traverse City to study at Northwestern Michigan College to be a pilot, but after he finished training, he ended up a building contractor and is active in the lumber business. Nick and Molly have two children, Megin and Joe (Joseph George).Megan has a son Isaac by her husband Peter Dressel.

Peg, our third daughter, married Rick Egelus from Cadillac. Rick also was part of the pilot program at Northwestern Michigan College. His father, Don Egelus, ran a shop in Cadillac and his stepmother was a schoolteacher. His mother owned a bar in Detroit but is now retired. They have three children, Patrick, Keegan, and Rory.

Kate (Kathleen Elizabeth), our fourth daughter, was named after a German forcign student my in-laws hosted at their farm, Kathryn Elizabeth Siemus from Monchengladbach, Germany. In fact, Elizabeth stood up for her when Kate was baptized. Kate was born on St. Patrick's Day. She married Amin, commonly called Moon, Nurmohamed, from Tanzania in East Africa. I've talked to Moon's father, Cameron, who tells me their ancestors came out of the Bombay area of India when East Africa was under British possession. The Indians were the business people in Tanzania until the revolution took place, and then many of them had to get out of there to save their lives. Moon's mother's name is Remti. His younger brother, Hassaan, entered the Minnesota Program for Agricultural Study and spent some time on our farm. He arranged for Moon to come to Northwestern Michigan College to study, which is how he and Kate met. They have three children, Naiven, Alia, and Jamal. Naiven has a daughter Zarah Beth and a son Kameron.

Our next daughter, Kerry Ellen, is married to Jamie Canellos of San Francisco, California. Kerry has done a lot of traveling and as a nurse could easily find employment most any place she wanted, but she ended up in San Francisco because she enjoys it there. She and Jamie were married there. They have a daughter, Claire.

Our youngest daughter, Bridget, is a graduate of Michigan State University in business and married Ron Popp from Leelanau County. The two of them have the Popp Excavating business in Traverse City. Bridget is actively involved in the bookkeeping end of their business. They have three children, Benjamin, Spencer, and Luke.

Three of our daughters are nurses: Kate, Kerry, and Peggy. Eight of the nine children attended Northwestern Michigan College for two years before they went onto something else. Two of the nurses have degrees from there. Peggy got married out of high school before she went to college and ended up getting her college degree in Georgia, where her husband Rick was training for helicopter training.

Matthew is a graduate of Michigan State University, John is a graduate of Ferris, Molly is a graduate of Arizona State University, and Lisa of Michigan State University. George needs a few credits yet to finish up his degree in horticulture from Michigan State University, but he attended there for several terms. While there, he was an aide in John Engler's office, so he too has some experience in the political process. Molly has been a county commissioner in Grand Traverse County, and all the kids have been active in our political campaigns, as have the in-laws, putting up signs and doing all the things necessary during an election.

As youngsters, our kids were always busy working on the farm. One of the advantages of raising a family on a farm is there's always plenty to keep people occupied, whether it's picking up rocks, hauling brush, pruning trees, hauling cherries, driving a tractor, pulling tarps, or whatever. There's always work to do, and I think my nine kids will tell you they got their share. You gain two ways: one they earn money; two they don't have time to spend it! In fact, my oldest daughter tells the story that when she was in college and some of her girlfriends were complaining about having to work to pay their tuition, she told them, "Don't feel bad—my dad had us work to pay our tuition through high school!"

A little hard work never hurt anybody, and I think the kids have all had a good background in not only working but in taking responsibility. Coupled with a good education, they've been able to go out in the world and take on their share of commerce and industry as well as their political responsibilities. They haven't had any trouble populating the world, and as of this date, Clara and I are proud to have twenty-three grandchildren and three great-grandchildren.

Chapter Eight
Politics and Humor

I never started out with the goal of becoming a state senator. I wanted to get married and raise a family, farm, and somehow reach retirement age with enough assets to carry me through to the end with perhaps a little something left for the children. After we retired from extension, Clara and I eventually found ourselves on the political scene. It was nothing we had planned; it was something that just came along.

When I think back over it, several things probably led to my being in the position I'm in today. For one thing, in the Great Depression, my father and my wife's father were Democrats in a highly Republican area. Lots of changes occurred in the period from 1935-1945 that the Democrats were on the leading edge of. Our parents were vitally interested and to a certain extent involved. They talked a lot about political issues. My dad kept a pretty close account of what the Republicans and Democrats were doing and FDR was a great inspiration to him.

The second thing is, as I mentioned earlier, both my parents and my wife's parents stressed the importance of maintaining a good reputation and of working hard. If you came up out of the Depression and were from a poor family, it was important that you attempted to "get ahead in the world" and try to improve your situation, which for many people was pretty bad. Being able to work with and communicate with others was simply a very important part of life.

John Hannah, the president of Michigan State University, always impressed me with one of his sayings: "The most important thing in life is people." If you feel this way, you automatically practice a term called "empathy," or being able to understand what it's like to walk in another person's shoes. Empathy is a learned skill, but not a taught one.

Perspective is also pretty important. I was always impressed by what was going on in foreign affairs from the standpoint of visitors I met who came from foreign countries. To date, I have visited Europe four times as well as China, Mexico, Chile, and Brazil. All those travels gave me a lot of perspective beyond the local arena.

In terms of elections, the first time I was involved was in the tenth grade, when I was elected president. In the eleventh grade, Clara was president, and then I was elected president again in the twelfth grade, so I had a little smattering of politics at the high school level. I wasn't involved politically in college, though I belonged to the Pomsters Club and Alpha Zeta, an honorary club.

When I got out of college, the local farmers immediately elected me to the Agricultural Stabilization Committee for the county; I was twenty-three years old. The two other members of the committee were both elderly gents, one Republican and one Democratic, so they elected me chairman of the local board as the neutral party.

I was also elected to the board of the Grand Traverse Cherry Producers Association by the cherry farmers in the county about the same time; it was several years before I assumed the chairmanship of that. I was plenty busy raising a family and working for extension and starting the farm and not really into politics all that much until 1970 or so, when 4-H agent Andy Olson came to me. Andy had been serving on the board of trustees of Northwestern Michigan College for several years, practically since its inception in about 1953. Northwestern Michigan College, the first community college in Michigan, is an extremely important educational as well as economic factor in Grand Traverse County and beyond.

Andy was retiring from the extension service and wanted to work for the college and could no longer serve as a trustee. He told me, "You've got to run for trustee to represent the rural areas on that board." He said, "I'll take your petitions around if you'll just agree to it."

I'd never really considered doing this, but I agreed. In those days in the extension service, we had to be non-partisan. We were under the Hatch Act and not allowed to take part in partisan activities, but this was a county-wide non-partisan election so it was okay.

I ran against Russell McNamara, the vice-president of the Traverse City State Bank, as well as a lady named June Janis from the Skegemog Lake area. As I recall, I got fifty-three percent of the vote against the other candidates and won that election. They always said afterwards that the next week McNamara was in a meeting talking to somebody in downtown Traverse City and said, "Where did he come from?" Apparently he hadn't recognized that our family had been in the county since 1867 and I was working with a lot of people in that county daily!

I was elected to fill out Andy's unexpired term, which meant I had to run again in 1972 and then in 1978 and 1984. I was elected four times to that college board in the county and I worked my way up to be vice-chairman over a twenty-year period. I never was chairman of the board. Les Biederman, one of the founders, was the first chairman I worked with, followed by Dr. Ted Kline and eventually followed by Jim Beckett; there may have been someone else in between. Harry Weitz was on the board as well as Julius Sleder and Alice Drulard and some others and then eventually Shirley Okerstrom and Bill Cunningham and Elaine Woods. I was replaced by my brother Mike, and my cousin Cheryl Gore, from the Carroll side, also served.

In 1982, when I retired from the Cooperative Extension Service, a lot of people figured I did it to run for the House of Representatives because Representative Mike Dively was moving on (he had replaced Arnell Engstrom). I might have been the logical person to run, but I'd never really given it a whole lot of thought. When I announced my retirement, I suddenly had a visit from Tom Power, who of course was involved at that time, along with a couple of others who were interested in what I was going to do. , Tom went ahead and ran and eventually was elected the representative from the 104th district. We worked together very closely during the time we were jointly in the legislature, from 1990-1992, before he retired and went to become a circuit court judge in Grand Traverse County.

John Engler was our senator at the time. He knew I was a Michigan Stater and he wanted to promote me for the position of MSU trustee. I was interested in that because I had been involved with Michigan State all my life. It's not only a great institution, it's particularly important to the agricultural community. I'd had experience as a community college trustee, so I thought this was logical except that I'd never been involved in any party politics. In fact, I'd kind of shied away from it. The Republican convention was in Mount Pleasant that year. John said, "Don't worry about it." I saw why after we got there. John engineered my getting on the ticket like the real professional he is.

I found myself on the ticket with Richard Headlee. Headlee was running for governor and I was running along with Laura Heuser for Michigan State University trustee.on the ticket We campaigned around the whole state, but Headlee lost that election to Jim Blanchard and so naturally the Democratic candidates for trustee won. Nonetheless, I got over 1,000,000 votes in the state, not bad for a beginner, but I thought that would probably be the end of my invasion into the partisan political area.

Upon my retirement from extension in 1982, I became very active in other organizations. I had been a Rotarian for several years, since about 1970, and the local club elected me to be their president for a year. As a result of that, I ended up on the board of Rotary Charities as a secretary for a little while.

I was elected president of the Traverse City Chamber of Commerce shortly after that and served in that capacity for a year. I was also on the board of directors of the First of America Bank, originally the Michigan National Bank in Traverse City, an organization I'd become involved with back in the early 1970s. My attorney, Stu Hubbell, had come to me one day and said, "How'd you like to be a bank director and bring a new bank into Traverse City?"

I hadn't thought about that either, but he had been involved with a couple other guys who had been interested in bringing Michigan National Bank into Traverse City and then changed their minds. He needed a couple of other people to go with him and bring in a de novo bank that would be turned over to the Michigan National Bank for a branch in Traverse City.

This idea was naturally heavily opposed by the other three banks in town, Traverse City State Bank, the National Bank, and the Empire Bank. When Empire Bank, under Jay Dutmers and then Lon Wilson, had first wanted to come into Traverse City, the other two banks had opposed that vigorously, but eventually Empire had received its charter and come in.

When we wanted to bring in Michigan National, the three of them ganged up on us. Stu and I traveled to Chicago to attend the federal hearings for the charter, while forty or fifty others went down to oppose it. We always said we considered that about even odds. We all rode the Blue Goose line out of Traverse City, and I remember the vice president of Traverse City State Bank, Charles Moorman, carrying my wife's bag on the plane. We were all from the same town and havin' quite a stew over the deal, but eventually we got the charter.

For a while, we had trouble getting a building. Bob Brick had a bicycle shop on Eighth Street and finally he sold us that building and we started the bank there. The people who had owned it before had a little grocery there and sold angleworms for fishing. They continued to live next door and the lady always kept a sign out in the yard, "Worms for Sale." She continued to put that sign in front of our bank; I think we were the only bank in Michigan with a sign in front that said we had worms for sale!

Michigan National also had a charter bank in Petoskey. They were out of Detroit and Lansing and eventually they sold their northern Michigan holdings to the First of America Bank in Kalamazoo. I served on the board of directors of the Traverse City Michigan National and then eventually on the First of America, who then sold to National City who decided to combine all their banks from Sault Ste. Marie to Manistee into one bank, with headquarters at Traverse City on Garfield Avenue. I served on that board until I was elected to the Senate in 1990, so I had a rather active period in the private sector, from 1982 to 1990.

In the fall of 1989, Shirley Okerstrom from the board of trustees of Northwestern Michigan College said to me one day, "How would you like to run for state senator?"

I said, "Well, I don't think I would."

"You should consider it," she said. "You'd be a good senator, and we need somebody from the 37th district to run against Senator Mitch Irwin."

Mitch is a good friend of mine and I didn't really get that excited about the prospect, but I found out later Shirley had been put up to asking me by Senator Connie Binsfeld. I've always said that women had the big influence on my life. Between the two of them, they stirred up Jim Dutmers from the Empire Bank and Bill Kurtz from Kurtz Music and others to try to talk me into running and I said, "Well, let's see how it goes."

In late November or early December, we went out to raise a few dollars. Things were coming in pretty good. My son George came home from Benton Harbor where he'd been farming with his father-in-law. As I mentioned, he'd worked in John Engler's office as an aide in college and he said, "Dad, I don't know whether you really want to do this. It's a lot of work and you don't really need it."

I thought maybe the best thing to do was turn them down and be done with it, so we gave the money back and went on about our business, because I had already arranged to take a horticultural tour in January of that year with Dr. Kesner to Australia and New Zeeland to visit the cherry orchards there.

We made that trip in late January and February of 1990. When we returned, that same group started in on me again, Dutmers and Kurtz and Shirley and a whole lot of different ones. Finally I made a trip to Lansing and talked to some of the Republican senators who were involved in the Michigan Senate. They gave me a lot of advice and encouragement. About ten days before the final filing date, I decided to go for it, even though I knew it would be a lot of work and I had a tremendous district to cover.

At the final hour on the final day to file, Mitch Irwin didn't file, which left an open seat. A man by the name of Weiss from Gaylord filed in his place. Suddenly, rather than running against an incumbent, I was running against someone else who was new to the electorate, which put us on a level playing field.

I've never known whether those Republican senators in the Michigan Senate had an inkling that Mitch wasn't going to run again. I suspect they did, because it's very, very difficult to beat an incumbent in office, yet they were convinced I would get his seat. In any event, when Mitch decided not to run, it made the job possible, or at least made it easier.

We ran a very tough primary first, because Bill Huber from Petoskey, Congressman Bob Davis' aide, had decided to run. Bill had been working the district on the northern part so he was well acquainted with all the Republicans in the U.P. and in some of the northern counties, but he hadn't worked Antrim and Grand Traverse counties, and Grand Traverse of course was the big county population-wise in the district.

I put better than 30,000 miles on the car from June to November getting around a district about the size of West Virginia that included five counties in the eastern U.P. and six counties below the bridge. It was 250 miles from my house to the other end of the district. At that time, Michigan was divided into thirty-eight senatorial districts to keep the population representation roughly the same.

After the 1990 census, the state was redistricted. The new 36th district consisted of eleven counties right around Traverse City. This meant it was now only sixty-five miles from my home to the farthest points of Roscommon and Manistee, a much more convenient district to drive.

In any case, in the 1990 campaign, I traveled through the upper part of the state and the eastern U.P. getting to know as many people as I could and what their needs and wishes were. Even though Bill took eight of the eleven counties, I took the majority of the vote with Grand Traverse County being as large as it was. Bill called to concede and compliment me that election evening about 10:30, and we have worked very closely together since. Patti Labelle and Virginia Watson as well as Suzanne Miller (now Allen) and Andy Anuzis and many others helped this neophyte through the campaigns.

In the general election, I ran against Tom Weiss of Gaylord, a Holiday Inn Motel operator. That was a close election because the district was fairly evenly balanced between Democrats and Republicans, neither of us was an incumbent, and both parties wanted the seat. It was a grueling battle, but I eventually won and went to Lansing.

The job of being a senator (and of course a representative would probably be the same thing) partly involves introducing, amending, and voting for or against legislation, but that is only a small part of the job. Committee meetings and gathering information and office calls and so on are other parts of the job. Working with the constituency back home, including weekend visits to various places, as well as being on the radio or in the newspaper or television, is probably the biggest part of the job.

Constituents expect their elected representatives to look out for their interests in terms of dealing with state agencies and departments. That probably takes more time, and maybe is more important, than legislation.

I consider representing people to be a very high calling in life. It's not particularly easy, and in fact it becomes very difficult when controversial issues are involved. As a legislator, we're expected to play Solomon and make decisions on issues that are sometimes not black and white.

Also, the facts of a case are not always accurately portrayed in the media. An interesting saying goes, "Perception is reality." That's a little different than the scientific method I learned. I was brought up to make decisions based on facts. As I tell many of my constituents, "When you get to the bottom line in business, in politics you're about halfway." I wouldn't really encourage anybody to set their sites on politics as a long-term career position, though it's necessary that people take an interest in it and step up to the plate when they can.

Politicians are often criticized and lampooned, but generally they're a reflection of the constituents they represent—or at least we hope they are. When we see a politician criticized for one thing or another, for the most part we have to assume we're criticizing the constituents that politician represents, because he is elected by a majority of the people who show up at the election and is probably doing the best he can to represent the interests of a majority of his constituents. By the same token, if a politician is praised for something, it's a reflection of the support his constituents have given him.

As a politician, I've tried to keep humor a very important part of my life. When I decided to run for the Michigan Senate, Gil Bogley, who was then a fellow Rotarian and good friend and the publisher of the *Record Eagle* in Traverse City, gave me a piece of advice: "George, I hope when you're finished with the Senate, you have the same sense of humor you did when you started." I've always kept that in mind when I've gotten into some of the situations I've encountered in government, such as debates on the Senate floor. I've found you can usually find a certain amount of humor in any situation.

Serving in the partisan politics in the Michigan Senate was a new world to me. It was the fastest thing I've ever done, in terms of the workload, and it wasn't only fast, there was lots of it. My time was divided between constituent relations, the media, time on the floor, and time on the committees. I was immediately put on the appropriations committee in charge of the agriculture and transportation budgets in the Senate and I was also put on the standing committees on agriculture and forestry, transportation, mental health, state police and military affairs, and public health. I found it a busy, intriguing, interesting, challenging place to be in my early sixties. One thing I had to quckly learn was "Perfect is the enemy of Good"

Certain things stick in your mind that probably don't add much to the official record that are nonetheless very interesting. I'll never forget the so-called fistfight in 1992 between Senators Gil DiNello and John Kelly. I was new and wondering what kind of place this Senate was going to be. In that first two years there were twenty Republicans and eighteen Democrats in the Senate, so it was fairly close. One day we were into a discussion on trying to cut taxes. That was the big issue all the way through the campaign and indeed through John Engler's administration. DiNello and Kelly had a big debate that got pretty heated. Both of them were on the Democratic side, Dinello being more conservative and very anti-tax and Kelly being more liberal.

I sat on the aisle at that time, and when the debate was over, Senator Kelly went up to the front to turn in some papers and DiNello was sitting on the aisle on the left side. He got up from his seat to shake hands as Kelly was coming down the aisle. I don't whether Kelly figured he was going to hit him or not, but Kelly took the first poke. As I've told many audiences in my district when I describe this fight, if those two ever get in the ring together, put your money on DiNello, because DiNello is a big Italian, about six feet tall with arms like a horse's leg. Kelly's a short, banty-rooster-Irishman type. He can do a lot of swinging, but all DiNello needed to do was throw his arms around him and hold him in place. The two of them went down on the floor and rolled under Senator Pridnia's desk and spilled his coffee and it got to be pretty hectic. Finally they got the sergeants and six other senators in and separated them and got the thing solved.

You would think the story ended there, but that wasn't the most interesting part of that little fracas. That came the next morning. Usually on the Senate floor you have anywhere from one to occasionally five television cameras periodically filming the goings on. The morning after the big fight, we came in to find no fewer than six television cameras ready for action. We all expected to see a big apology, and though each of them got up and gave an impassioned, long-winded dissertation on what had happened, in neither of their soliloquies did I hear the word "apology" or "apologize." I noted two things: the media was more interested in a potential apology than in any real work on the floor, and those two senators were able to get up and talk quite a while without actually saying anything. I couldn't help but wonder how a body could dance around the head of a pin for that long!

One of the most interesting votes we took during that period was the vote on the Good Samaritan bill, necessary to keep insurance costs down and allow doctors and others to treat patients brought into the hospital from accidents. This involved an exercised debate with the Republicans primarily on the "Yes" side and the Democrats primarily on the "No" side. Connie Binsfeld, the lieutenant governor, was running things that day. After the debate, we had sixty seconds to vote.

Because Senator Cruce had resigned, thirty-seven senators were serving, which meant we required nineteen votes to pass the proposition. We began to vote, the clock running down and the Republicans primarily voting "Yes" until we had eighteen votes up on the board and the Democrats had seventeen "No" votes. We were down to about the last five seconds and Senator Carl, a Republican from Macomb County, had not yet voted. I fully expected him to cast the nineteenth "Yes" vote, but for some reason or another he cast a "No," which left a tie of eighteen to eighteen. Well, a rousing cheer went up from the Democrat side of the aisle, but they had apparently forgotten that in the event of a tie, the lieutenant governor votes. Her "Yes" would give us the nineteenth vote and the issue would pass, which is what happened. I think it's the one few times she voted during that two-year period.

The Democrats had also forgotten that if one of their "No" voters had been on the ball, the minute Carl cast his vote, making it a tie, if they had pulled up their button on the voting machine so that they did not cast a vote, in other words becoming a not-voting statistic, then the final score would have been eighteen to seventeen. In that case, the lieutenant governor would not have voted and the issue would not have passed. These are some of the intriguing items that make being a senator so challenging and of such interest to me.

Another interesting vote dealt with the so-called teachers' anti-strike legislation. Previously, teachers could strike and continue to get paid while on strike though other union workers could not. Legislation was introduced that said teachers on strike likewise wouldn't receive pay. This was hotly contested in the House of Representatives and the Republicans needed one more vote to pass the bill. At midnight, the clock would run out and all would be lost. Representative Bill Bobier (pronounced "Bo-beer") was in Belize celebrating his twenty-fifth wedding anniversary with no means of communication, but he and his wife were to arrive at the Detroit airport the night of the vote shortly before eleven p.m. Arrangements were made for a fast pick-up and trip to the capitol. He made it with seconds to spare, and I have encapsulated the event in the poem below.

The Midnight Ride of Bill Bobier

Listen my children and you shall hear
Of the midnight ride of Bill Bobier.
It was the thirteenth of April in '94
If I've got you interested, I'll tell you more.
Our hero turned famous that fateful day,
Changed the course of history, some people say.

The Republicans were short one vote on HB 5128
Time was running out; the night getting late.
At midnight the Democrats would take over with a smile
And the bill would end up in the Number 13 file.

Speaker Hillegonds says,
"Where's Bobier? Is he in the trees?"
"No," they reported, "he's down in Belize."
But another report said he's on his way home.
Says Paul, "We need him here under the Dome.
Is he coming by land or coming by sea,
And on what shore will he shortly be?"

"Neither," they said. "He's coming by air
And into Detroit if the weather is fair."

Down from the plane and into the ramps
Came Bill and his wife, looking like tramps.
T-shirts, sandals, straw hats, and shorts—
What do you expect of tourists and sports?
Hoffman and Mann threw Bill in the back
And Phil and Trish took care of Pat.

Out of the airport at a cool 85
To Lansing we'll be in an hour and five.
"Not fast enough" said Mann; "Put her to the floor!"
And soon they were doing 104!

Sleet or snow, rain or shine,
The vote will be there by 11:59.
Past Brighton and Howell, on 96 they sped
Not a cop in sight, or their budget was dead!
Fowlerville, Webberville, past country and farm,
On they came without raising alarm.

Back at the Dome the Dems were ecstatic,
The MEA in the balcony was being sarcastic.
"We'll strike as we like and still get paid!"
They gloated and bragged, "We've got it made!"
The Dems were all smiling, "To heck with the kids!
More money and more taxes will be our bids!"

But, unknown to those inside,
Our hero arrived with a slip and a slide.
11:52, no time to spare,
The voting had started amid the gong and the glare.
Up the elevator and onto the floor
Charged the Oceana farm boy with confidence galore.

Suddenly a hush as reality set in.
Dems glared in scorn; Republicans grinned.
Young Bill, all tanned and unshaven alas
Would cast the one vote to make the bill pass.
He voted at 11:59 and up went a cheer.
He should have been named "Legislator of the Year!"

You know the rest in the books you have read,
How the tide was turned, the naysayers fled.
K-12 education in Michigan was saved
By Engler and Hillegonds and Bobier's escapade.

Through history to the last,
In hours of darkness, peril, and need,
People will count on public servants like Bill
To get the job done, no matter what speed.
Right will prevail through work and sacrifice,
But sometimes it helps to add a little spice.

You may all recall Paul Revere's ride,
But with his luck, I'll take Bobier on my side.

One needs to maintain a sense of humor in order to serve amicably and admirably in the Senate. Certain senators seem to manage that, each in their own way. In 1992, Senator Phil Hoffman came into the Senate. He had been in the House of Representatives for several years and was pretty well acquainted with the legislative process. He knew we had a custom that when a senator passed his first bill, he needed to treat the rest of the senators with a little token. I remember when I passed my first bill, I gave each senator a four-ounce package of dried cherries. Hoffman knew the custom, so he came in the day his first bill was up with a box of breakfast goodies, donuts and that type of thing, and put it in the cloakroom.

When the session began, he got up and asked permission to make an announcement. When it was granted, he told everyone that since his first bill was going to pass today, he'd brought in some goodies and everybody should help themselves. We all thanked him and went on with the session. Eventually his bill came up and passed. Then Senator Phil Arthhultz, the floor leader and very accomplished at that, got up grinning and said he wanted permission to make an announcement. After it was granted, he went on to say that the custom of the Senate was that *after* a new senator had passed a bill, he was expected to provide a little token to the rest of the senators. It really didn't count if he did it beforehand, so we should all expect a token from Senator Hoffman the next morning also!

Undoubtedly the most significant issue in my first four years in the Senate was Proposal A on school finance. In the final hours of a long session that extended to December 24, we worked a twenty-six-hour marathon to put that package together. By the time I was home and rested, Christmas Eve was gone and we were into Christmas Day of 1993. That was a very significant piece of legislation and a turning point in the whole issue of taxing property as related to school operations.

I love a good story, and I'm glad to say my years in public service were good for a lot of them. One time Roy Gummerson in the extension service was telling about the Finlander from the U.P. who went to Hawaii. When the Finn got off the plane, he came down the ramp and a Hawaiian girl met him and put a lei around his neck and said, "Aloha from Hawaii."

He put out his hand to shake hers and said, "Ahola from Pelky."(a little town in the U.P.)

Representative Dave Anthony from Escanaba told me the story of Toivo, the Finn who was on the stand in court. Toivo had been in an accident and at the time of the accident had indicated he didn't have any injuries. Later, he decided to sue to collect insurance for being injured in the accident. The lawyer for the other side said to him, "Now, Toivo, yes or no, were you injured at the accident?"

Toivo said, "Well, it's not quite that simple. There's a little more to the story than that."

The lawyer said, "We don't need all of that. Just say yes or no. You said at the accident you weren't injured. Now you're suing for injury. Yes or no, were you injured at the accident?"

"You've got to let me tell the whole story," Toivo said.

"We just need to know yes or no," repeated the lawyer.

Toivo said, "I can't say yes or no. I have to tell you how it all happened."

Finally the lawyer gave in and Toivo told the story. "I was driving up the road in my pickup with my cow, Meiko, in na back. We come 'roun da corner and there was a big logging truck coming from dudder direction. And too late we didn't see it and hit head on in na crash, which trew me into da woods and my cow Meiko onto da road. As luck would have it, just about that time two troopers came along in the state police car, stopped, got out, and I heard one of them say to the other, 'This cow is in bad shape. We're goin' to have to shoot her.' And bang! The gun went off. About that time I come stumblin' out of the woods and the trooper turned around with the gun pointed at me and still smokin' and said, 'How do you feel?' And I said to him, 'I feel just fine; no trouble at all!'"

Another joke I like involves some big-whig coming up to my place to visit me. I take him out in the pickup for a drive around the country. We get out to Toivo Mackey's farm and Toivo is out in the yard. We look around and see a little building with some smoke comin' out the chimney, which I immediately recognize as a sauna. Outside the sauna are several men from the community with their clothes off ready to go inside. It looks kind of funny, so I say to Toivo, "What's going on here?"

Toivo says, "Oh, it's a festival we have here every now and then. The women from the community are all inside blindfolded and the men go in one at a time. The first man to be identified gets the prize. By the way, who have you got here with you in the pickup?"

You happen to be honoring some big politician from Lansing or something, so you say, "It's so and so,like the director of agriculture for the state of Michigan."

To which Toivo replies, "Well, it's a good thing you got here. His name's been called three times already!"

One of the best stories I ever heard out of the extension service was told by Woodie Varner, the state extension director back in the early '50s. Woodie was a Texan who liked to tell quite a few stories to illustrate a point. When he came into the extension service at MSU, he decided to make several changes to the way things were run. Of course the extension agents, used to operating under a certain system with a certain set of guidelines for many years, tended to resist change. They didn't necessarily mind promoting change for somebody else, but when it came to changing their own modus operandi, that took a little doing. In such cases you can either resist or stall, and Woodie knew he needed to get the agents in a frame of mind to go along with his ideas. When the annual conference was held and the whole staff was gathered, Woodie delivered his message and then asked, "Are there any questions from the audience?"

One old fellow, a county agent, stood up in the back of the room and started to tell this new director from Texas how far off-base he was and how his new ideas were certainly not anything anybody ought to take seriously and how he for one didn't intend to implement any of them.

To which the director of extension then said, "Is there anyone else in the room with thirty years of service and two oil wells who would like to make a comment?"

One of the finest humorous moments that ever happened to me within the service occurred early in my career. The extension agents in northern Michigan used to gather for a day once a year at the Ralph McMullen DNR training center at Higgins Lake. We'd drive over in the morning and have a series of meetings until noon, then have lunch, then continue with our meetings. We always tried to get back home by supper time or so. In those days, a few of the home demonstration agents, Edna (Deo) Alsup from Traverse City, Jeannette Shadko from Beulah, and Emma Reinbold from Petoskey, were sitting in the middle of the room knitting. Years later, one of the directors passed the rule that they couldn't knit when someone was speaking. I guess he thought that made speakers nervous, but they used to knit pretty regularly in those days. They figured they might as well be doing something productive while the speakers were going on.

Emma, great lady that she was, had a wooden leg. I don't know whether she was born with a missing leg or not, but she always had a wooden leg and nobody thought too much about it. She got around about as good with that as with a regular leg. One day it was getting pretty close to noon and we had a comment period. Ed Kidd was the county agricultural agent from Cheboygan. His county had a lot of timber in it and he didn't think we were putting enough emphasis on education in the forestry aspect of our work, so he got up and started pontificating on the value of the forest industry to the state of Michigan and the northern part of the state and the fact that we ought to be doing more educating on the proper methods of handling the forests. Of course, the longer he talked, the more carried away he got. He made the mistake of stopping to draw a breath and out of a clear blue sky, Emma spoke up and said, "That's right, Ed. Give it to 'em. If it wasn't for the wood industry, some us wouldn't have a leg to stand on!"

Everybody loved Emma. She was such a great lady and had a great sense of humor and quite often it involved that wooden leg. Her comment broke up the meeting and sent everybody over to the cafeteria for lunch.

Another story involves Emma going into the J.C. Penney store one day to buy a garter. She said to the clerk, "I'd like to buy one garter."

The clerk said, "Don't you need a pair of garters?"

Emma said, "No, I hold the other stocking up with a thumb tack."

Edna Alsup, the home agent in Grand Traverse County with whom I worked for many years, also had a great sense of humor. I don't know what the subject was exactly one time, but we got on the subject of people who do a lot of talking. Of course Edna and I both knew the value of listening, but Edna had a favorite cliché, which I've used many times: "We learn by listening, and it's hard to listen if you're doin' all the talking!"

A horticultural story I like is about the farmer who took a load of apples in and had them processed and sold. When he got done, his broker said, "Well, the apples didn't bring enough money for me to pay you anything. In fact, you owe me a little bit, but if you bring in one of those chickens I saw out in your barnyard the other day for my Sunday dinner, we'll call it even."

The next day the farmer came in with a gunnysack and dumped two chickens on the broker's desk. The broker said, "Well, that's mighty fine of you, but you really only owe me one chicken."

The farmer said, "Yah, but I've got another load of apples outside."

There are certain similarities between extension and legislative work in terms of serving constituents and helping them solve problems. In the extension service, the whole idea is to help farmers help themselves, rather than make decisions for them. The idea is to provide the latest research information from MSU and other agricultural colleges in the United States, as well as the USDA, and then allow people to make up their own minds about what to do. It goes without saying that once in a while a farmer comes in to talk about a question, and after you provide him with the latest information and various alternatives, he steps over to the office door and closes it and says something like, "Now that we've got this door closed and you don't have to be in your official capacity, tell me which way you'd go" and try to get you to make the final decision for him.

In the legislature, you not only look at the latest information and the constituencies' desires, you also have to come up with alternative solutions to problems. After that's done, you have to make a decision and vote yes or no. Most of the time, you've got just sixty seconds to punch either the red or green button, so there is a difference from that standpoint!

Also, in terms of the legislature, thanks to the budget, you have a little more power to actually get things done. Some of the bureaucracy is pretty well entrenched in state government. Certain bureaucrats have been there a long time and have seen politicians come and go. Thus, they aren't always as responsive to needs as they might be. But many of the departments are very cooperative, and if they can get a problem solved, they often work with the legislator to do so.

Chapter Nine

Family Fun on a Trip to Ireland

Before I was elected to the legislature, my cousin John Gallagher said to me one time, "We ought to go to Ireland." He wanted to visit because Leo, his uncle, a veteran of World War II, had kept track of relatives there. He knew I'd traveled to Europe with Clara to see our oldest daughter, Lisa Jane. We'd also had some foreign students on our farm out of a program from the University of Minnesota, notably Norbert Arnegger from Ravensburg, Germany. We'd also traveled to Belgium to visit friends in the fruit processing business, Albert Heymans and his sons, so we agreed to go.

The family in Ireland we were most familiar with had the last name of O'Kane. Patrick O'Kane was the cousin we knew most about (his mother was a Gallagher), but there was also his brother Jim and several nephews, Seamus and Sean and so on.

When we got to Ireland, we learned that Patrick's wife Una was also an O'Kane, so it's an O'Kane married to an O'Kane, but they're not related by blood. We also discovered that one of the nieces of the O'Kanes married a Gallagher, but they weren't related, either.

"O'Kane" is the English translation of "O'Caithin," which is the Gaelic or Irish version of the name. Nephew Seamus O'Kane is a professor at University College, Dublin, and a specialist in the Gaelic language who speaks it fluently. In charge of the archives department there, he is working to preserve the Irish language.

We made the decision to go to Ireland the one spring, and I said I'd make the reservations. I encouraged John to get ahold of his relatives and let them know we were coming and he said he would do that. I saw him a couple of times at church during the summer and asked if he'd done it. He said he hadn't, but he soon would.

In September, we got on the plane in Traverse City to fly to Ireland and I said to him, "Did you get ahold of your relatives? Do they know we're comin' and are we welcome?"

He said he still hadn't gotten to it yet but he had their address and the town they were from and he'd take care of it when we got to Ireland. Okay, I thought, so we flew to Dublin and stayed overnight and then rented a car to drive to northern Ireland, the part that's under British rule.

The first thing we had to do was learn to drive a car on the wrong side of the road. The Irish as well as the British drive on the opposite side of the road that we do in the United States. John's relatives, the O'Kanes, lived in the little hamlet called Dooish, just outside the village of Drumquin, not far from Omagh, the county seat of County Tyrone in Northern Ireland. So we traveled to Omagh and got a hotel room for the night and went down to the restaurant to have dinner.

On the way into the hotel, we noticed a hole in the glass in the door panel. It looked for all the world like a bullet hole, and though we were assured it had gotten there by some other means than the big British army base next door, I still think it was a bullet hole. We sat down for dinner and John said to the waitress, "We'd like to get ahold of Patrick O'Kane."

The waitress went over to the desk and had the girl call for Patrick O'Kane. Pretty soon she came back and told John to go talk to his cousin. He came back a few minutes later and said it was the wrong Patrick O'Kane, but the man knew the right Patrick O'Kane and would get ahold of him and he'd call us back.

It wasn't long before the phone rang. John went over, and when he came back I said, "Was that the right one?"

He said, "Ya, that was my cousin."

Sure enough, we were to pay him a visit at ten o'clock the following morning in the village of Dooish, though I can't really call Dooish, of Dooish Mountain, a village; it's more of a hamlet.

There was a time when the British had a ruling in Ireland that Catholics could not build a church on top of a hill. They didn't want the belfry and cross to show. Instead, Catholic churches had to be built in the valleys. Dooish sits in kind of a valley, and its St. Patrick's Catholic Church was built during that time. Over at the neighboring parish, Dromare, originally the home parish of the O'Kanes, the church is built in the valley all right, but the cemetery is on a high hill, and at the upper end of the cemetery sits the bell tower. The rule didn't say Catholics couldn't build a bell tower at the top of the hill; it just said they couldn't build a *church* at the top of the hill.

At Dooish, we met some of the finest people I've ever known, Pat and Una O'Kane and their children Rory, Jerrad, Sinead, and Monica, along with two of Una's sisters, Sheila and Briad, which I suppose is a form of Bridget. Sheila and Briad were retired nurses. They had taken nurse's training as young women and then worked in Liverpool, England, throughout their lives. Upon retirement, they'd moved back to the village, where they'd built a nice cottage.

Since the time of the British ruling, a new church has been built in Dooish on some land donated by Patrick O'Kane near Sheila and Briad's cottage because the old church needed to be replaced. The old church was essentially left to stand until it fell. We learned it's pretty difficult to take down some of those Irish churches because the cemeteries are built all the way around them.

We couldn't come out the night we arrived because they were having a three-day retreat put on by the Passionest Fathers out of Dublin in southern Ireland. After we met these long-lost relatives, we attended services with them for the next two days. The first morning we went to mass, the villagers were courteous and nodded but there wasn't any conversation, although it was obvious to everyone that strangers were in town. We also noticed in church that the older generation had a habit of the men sitting on one side and the women on the other. This was apparently a custom many, many years ago in the Catholic Church in Ireland, and probably in other parts of the world as well.

We attended a sermon one night in which the young priest gave a talk on justice. I thought to myself, "It's going to be interesting to hear an Irish priest talk about justice in northern Ireland." He went through the usual lesson about the fact that the just man gives adequate work for his pay and the just owner gives adequate pay for the work and so on. He finally got to the climax of the sermon and said that we needed to be just on everything but taxes!

Gallagher jabbed me in the ribs with his elbow on that one, but I thought to myself that it was probably true, that if the British were collecting the taxes and the Irish were paying them, there's some question about what constitutes justice in that situation.

The next day while we were walking down the sidewalk, we met that young priest and we had to kid him a bit. We told him we were interested in his sermon, especially the part about the taxes.

He remarked, "Every sermon has to have a little jolt." He got to talking with us about who we were and where we were from, and that morning when we went to mass he mentioned we were visitors from Michigan who grew cherries and we were relatives of the O'Kanes. After that, all the villagers, friends, and neighbors of the O'Kanes wanted to talk to us and they really opened up, but they weren't about to do it until they got the okay from up front.

We spent many good days in Ireland. They had an interesting armed camp situation at the time. When you crossed the border from southern Ireland to Northern Ireland, you had to go through a checkpoint. One day I was making out an envelope and I put "Northern Ireland" on the address. Briad said to me, "Why do you put in the 'Northern'? There's only one Ireland!"

The British don't feel that way about it, which explains their checkpoints. The other thing that's more distressing is the local Ulster constabulary, made up of local volunteers. These people are fellow farmers, and anyone who cares to sign up for a short stint in law enforcement is paid for their time. It's a little bit like fightin' forest fires used to be in the western United States. The problem is, when you do it that way, some of the people getting paid to fight the fires are the ones setting them in the first place!

It's a little bit that way with the Irish Ulster Constabulary. They have the privilege of stopping traffic on the road and searching cars. The Irish watch pretty closely to see to it that one set doesn't drop something in the trunk and then, when they're stopped further on down the road, they get picked up for something they didn't put there in the first place. Anyone can sign up for that constabulary duty and get paid, but Catholics don't sign up for it. Consequently, the constabulary is made up mostly of Orangemen. That makes a very distressing situation because the same neighbor you might be farming alongside of today or going to the auction sale with or being a good friend of may be a uniformed cop stopping you on the road and searching your car the next day.

We got stopped one night. We'd been to a party up at Sean O'Kane's in Drumquin singing and dancing. About midnight, we headed back to Dooish. We came around the bend of the road and saw six flashlights. There's always one constable posted in front and two on each side and one behind. Gallagher had drunk a couple of toddies and he rolled down the window and in a loud voice said, "Havin' your fun?"

Bernadine quieted him down and once they saw my tourist passport they immediately waved us on. They're not interested in harassing tourists; they're just interested in checking out the local gentry.

It was a great trip for us, meeting those friends and relatives of the Gallaghers. Clara and I've been back there since on a trip with our daughters Lisa and Kerry. The four of us visited them, and then their two boys Rory and Gerard came back to the United States and spent some time with us on the farm. Rory turned out to be a very excellent young man. He took diving instructions in Traverse City and eventually in New Jersey and finally under a program with the British, so he's an accomplished diver. He spent some time in the Persian Gulf working on the oil rigs and eventually married a girl from Traverse City, Gina Wambold, and worked the oil rigs down off the Gulf of Mexico, working out of Louisiana. Now he lives in Traverse City.

There are two colleges in Dublin, Trinity College, which is a little better known, and University College. I suppose it's a little bit like the University of Michigan and Michigan State. We got to know our nephew Seamus, in charge of the archives, pretty well. His wife is from Sweden and they have two children. In their home he speaks Gaelic, she speaks Swedish, and the kids learn English in the street, so they were accomplished in three languages by the time they went to school.

Clara happened to mention to Seamus, who is kind of a humorist, that her grandmother was a McGarry (we also visited one of her Umphry relatives at Milltown in the county of the Armagh). The

McGarrys were from French Park, in County Roscommon, and Seamus was prompted to tell us about the Roscommon sheep stealers. Many, many years ago, people drove their sheep through County Roscommon. There were stone walls on each side of the road in a certain section, and no matter how closely you guarded your sheep, you never ended up with the number you started out with. In fact, Seamus said only one person from Roscommon ever went to Heaven, and they caught him leaving with the Lamb of God under his arm!

Patrick O'Kane had a brother, old Uncle Jim, who lived with his wife on the home farm in County Tyrone. They didn't have any children. Patrick and his children and family had taken the pledge and were the kind of Irish who don't take anything to drink, but Uncle Jim hadn't taken the pledge. We spent one night on the farm with Uncle Jim and he told us about many of the things that go on in that particular area. One was that the British have a system of promoting agriculture in which they pay subsidies for the numbers of animals. Uncle Jim's comment was, "You'd be surprised how many times you can put a sheep through the countin' chute.

He told us that one time he'd had to put a British hunting party off his land. We thought it was interesting but just a passing comment until we got to talkin' to Seamus, who one day said, "Did Uncle Jim tell you how he put the British off his land?"

"No," we answered.

"When the Irish were able to get their land back several years ago from the British, in many cases, the British kept the hunting rights. So the Irish passed the law that they had to have the permission of the present owner of the property in order to hunt. Uncle Jim was out on his property one day and he caught this British party hunting without the proper permission, so he said, "Ye'll be off.and Ye'll not be walkin' on Irish soil while you're doin' it, so off with your shoes and into the creek and down the creek to the road,' which they did."

Gallagher said, "Well, if it was a huntin' party, seems as though they might have given Uncle Jim a little trouble."

Seamus said, "Uncle Jim had his shotgun handy in case anybody tried anything!"

On that same trip we visited Donegal, Connemara, Galway, and down around the Ring of Kerry before we left Ireland to go to France and eventually Germany. When we were going through the Ring of Kerry, Bernadine and Clara Bell noticed a sign for Kerry Woolen Mills. We drove down a little country road and into a farmyard. Nobody was around, so we got out and went over to the barn door and peaked in and saw a crew working. We were at the actual mill! We got pretty well acquainted with the owner and ended up buying some blankets to ship home for the kids. It was one of the last mills in Ireland using water power to weave the wool. They did their own dying and made the blankets and other woolen goods right there at the mill.

We hadn't planned to buy blankets and the owner didn't take credit cards. Settling this was going to take up a sizeable chunk of our cash and we were trying to figure out what to do when the man said, "Well, do you have a personal check?"

That kind of surprised me, and I said, "Sure."

"Just make me out a check for it. I'll charge it to you in Irish pounds."

I said, "Do you need references or my drivers license?" That's the usual situation.

His answer was, "For what?"

I wrote him out a check and Gallagher did the same. Afterwards, I got to thinking about it. He had to package and ship those blankets, and I expect the check cleared the bank before he put them on the plane to send them to the United States. It was a good deal for us, and we got well acquainted with the man and he told us a lot of interesting history about that particular mill.

One of the best stories was that a prior owner had installed electricity. Originally the electricity was made from a dam on the river, but public electricity was brought in some years later. For years, the owner drew off the public electricity in the daytime and at night switched his own power into the line, which reversed the meter. It took about three years for the authorities to catch on!

Later in life, when my attorney Stu Hubbell, an Irishman and a good friend of mine, and retired U.S. Senator Bob Griffin from the state supreme court were going to make a trip to Ireland together with their wives, I told them some of the places we went to that I thought would be of interest, including the Kerry Woolen Mill.

Afterwards, Stu told me they stopped there and had quite a conversation with the fellow. He remembered Gallagher and me, that we'd been a couple of cherry growers who'd bought some blankets from him. He also told me the mill owner had said to them, "What do you two do for a living?"

Hub told him they were both lawyers. He said the mill owner looked at him and said, "Couldn't make it honest, eh?"

Talking about U.S. Senator Bob Griffin also reminds me of the time President Gerald Ford came to Traverse City to be the grand marshal of the National Cherry Festival parade. Douglas Gallagher, John's youngest brother, was on the home farm out on North Long Lake Road. Doug and Joann had a bunch of kids who wanted to go to the parade and see President Ford, and Doug said, "Well, we've got to make hay today. We're not going to have time to do that, but I'll guarantee you'll get as close to President Ford as anybody else in the parade if you'll just do what I tell you."

They worked all morning and came in for lunch at noon and Doug said, "Make up some signs saying 'Welcome, President Ford.'" He knew Senator Griffin had a cabin at Long Lake, west of the Gallagher's place. He'd read in the newspaper about the parade and that President Ford was going to be a guest of Senator Griffin out at his cabin at Long Lake. That meant the cavalcade would be passing right by the Gallagher farm. About the time he knew the parade was over, Doug told the kids to get out by the road with their signs and then he stationed his wife south of the road at the gate of the cattle pasture. Doug had about a hundred Holstein cows pastured on the south side of the road, and every day at milking time they opened the gate and put those cows across the road to the barn on the north side to be milked.

Doug said they waited until the state police came through first and cleared all the roads and blocked all the side roads and the helicopters went overhead. As soon as the helicopters were past, Doug said to Joanne, "Turn 'em loose." He put one hundred head of cattle on North Long Lake Road just as the presidential cavalcade came up over the hill and it stopped them dead center. Ford was probably about fifteen or twenty feet from Doug's kids, who were waving excitedly at him. Doug said the secret service jumped out of the car with their hands on their holsters looking up at the top of the silo like there might be a bunch of commies around and said, "Get them cows out of the road."

Doug said, "Well, they'll be out of the road when they get to the other side."

It didn't bother Ford any. He'd been around Grand Rapids dairy farms long enough to know what was going on, and he got a big kick out of it. In fact, he was wavin' happily at the kids.

The statewide papers, the *Detroit Free Press* and the *News* and the *Grand Rapids Press* all picked up on the story and had a picture of it. One headline was, "Herd of Cows Inadvertently Stops Presidential Cavalcade." (I think they were intimating we were a hick town up north) Well, there wasn't anything inadvertent about it. It was very carefully planned and executed.

Doug went down to the J & S in town for a cup of coffee the next morning and was talking about it and one of the sheriff's deputies said, "You can't do that. That's the president of the United States."

Doug replied, "I not only can, I already have."

Chapter Ten

A Few Personal Profiles and Various Final Stories

One of the more outstanding people on the peninsula who lived to be one hundred years old and more was Rose Kroupa Dohm. Rose had a farm in the Ogdensburg neighborhood just across the road from the cemetery. One of the interesting things that happened in extension was the opportunity to visit with her one day. It all came about rather strangely. I was in my office in the first part of June, toward the end of my career, when I got a telephone call from the National Cherry Festival office in Traverse City. The biggest local event of the year, several hundred thousand people attend the activities and each year the parade features a marshal of national significance. As mentioned, President Ford has been the parade marshal as well as many other national and international figures. One time I brought a French cherry farmer over by the name of Lucien Ginoux to be our international parade marshal.

This particular year, the festival had arranged to have Colonel Sanders of Kentucky Fried Chicken fame be the parade marshal, but about the first of June, he backed out very suddenly. With the festival fewer than thirty days off, the festival committee was looking for a parade marshal. They had a meeting that morning and decided they'd like to have the oldest cherry farmer in the county be the parade marshal. They called me up in my position as extension director, or as most of them would call it the agricultural agent, to see if I knew who the oldest cherry farmer was. I said I did. They wanted to know if I thought I could get him to be the parade marshal for the festival.

I said, "Well, I don't know. It's not a him, it's a her that's the oldest cherry farmer in the county. She lives on the peninsula. She's one hundred years old and her name is Rose Dohm." I told them to give me a few days.

Rose farmed with her son Fred, or Frederick, and her grandson Freddy. I called out to Fred Dohm's house and told him what I wanted and asked if he thought she would do it.

He said, "Why don't you come out and ask her?"

That sounded reasonable, so I went out that afternoon. When I got to the farm, Frederick and Freddy were in the barn doing some repair work. It was kind of a rainy day, so we talked a little bit and pretty soon Fred said, "Let's go up to the house. Ma's taking her nap."

I went into the living room while he went into the bedroom where Rose was lying on the bed. She was a real small woman at that time, probably not much more than five feet tall and maybe a little less. Fred said to his mother, "Ma, Mr. McManus is here to see you. He's got something he wants to ask."

She got up and came over and sat down next to me on the couch and turned up her hearing aid and said, "Which McManus are you?"

"I'm George." That didn't impress her much, so I said, "George was also my dad." That didn't impress her either, so then I said, "Arthur McManus was my grandfather."

"Oh," she said, "Which Arthur McManus?"

"Little Art. My grandfather was Little Art."

"I knew him," she said. "He used to come to the dances at Bowers Harbor."

Apparently there used to be a dance hall on the second floor of a grocery store just south of what is now a restaurant at Bowers Harbor. Rose was born and raised just north of Bowers Harbor in the Neahtawanta area and my grandfather was born just to the south on Devils Dive Road, so it would be logical that they would have attended the same dances. That's not to be confused with the other dance hall on Old Mission that the Hills sisters ran, which was also a dance floor on the second floor over a grocery store in the Old Mission area.

After Rose had identified me as part of the peninsula and an acceptable character to talk to, she said, "What is it that you want?"

"We'd like to have you be the parade marshal for the National Cherry Festival this year."

"How far do I have to walk?" she asked.

"You wouldn't have to walk at all," I said. "We would give you a ride in the car."

She promptly got off the couch and walked over to her son, Frederick, who was in his seventies at the time. She said, "Fred, do you think we could take the afternoon off and go to the parade?"

Fred said, "Ya, Ma. I think it would be all right if we took the afternoon off."

She came back and sat down next to me and said, "Young man, if it'll help you out, I'll do it."

Parade day came and the arrangements were made. I decided I'd better be the chauffeur and drive the car that would carry Rose through the parade so I could look after her. Various members of the family bought her some new clothes and got her all dolled up. The parade was at two o'clock in the afternoon in those days and at noon there was always the governor's luncheon. Bill Milliken from Traverse City was the governor of Michigan and I knew Bill pretty well. He and his wife Helen were at the luncheon at the Park Place Hotel and I went over to their table and said, "Governor, I'm going to be driving Rose Dohm as parade marshal of the festival today. Rose is a cherry farmer from the peninsula and she's over a hundred years old. It would be nice if you and Helen could come by the car at the beginning of the parade and say hello." We always lined up for the parade on Railroad Avenue and dignitaries like the governor and senators and representatives were the first to lead the parade in those days, with the marshal right behind them, so I knew the governor would be within a block or so of where we'd be.

He said, "Sure. If we get a chance, we'll do that."

We lined up for the parade a little ahead of two o'clock. It was a hot day and we had the air conditioner on. Rose was kind of a short woman and she was barely stickin' up over the dashboard. I looked up and saw Bill and Helen Milliken walking up to find us. When they got near the car, I pushed the electric button and rolled the window down. Bill stuck his hand in and said, "Hello, Rose. How are you?"

She couldn't see too well, but she looked up when she heard his voice and said, "Billy Milliken, is that you? I remember the day you were born. I was up to the hospital when your mother delivered you. Glad to see you here."

When I saw the governor afterwards, he said, "She's a pretty perky gal, isn't she?"

Rose had farmed all her life, and when she got too old to handle the farm herself, she turned it over to her son, Fred, who by now had practically turned it over to his son. But she always maintained ownership and farmed on a 50-50 share-proposition with Frederick. She ran her own affairs and she loaned out money to family members. I remember Fred coming into the office one time to talk about buying forty acres. I think that acreage included the farm his daughter, Virginia Coulter, lives on now. He wanted to know what I thought about that piece and whether it was worth the money. We talked about it for some time and I remember him saying, "Well, I wouldn't have any trouble getting' the money. I could just go to Ma and borrow it." I think Fred was probably better than sixty years old at the time, but they still did business in a business-like manner, even though it was mother and son.

That was not completely unusual in those days, as I indicated earlier. My grandparents on the Fromholz side each kept their own set of books. Grandpa kept his and Grandma kept hers and they farmed together, but the ownership of their property was separate for many, many years.

Rose Dohm was very significant. She came from an old family, of course. The Kroupas are a large family on the peninsula and she came out of that clan and was connected with the fruit business all her life. She was a very hard worker and a good businesswoman and I was proud to see that she got to be the parade marshal one year for the National Cherry Festival. I for one didn't miss Colonel Sanders at all.

Rose Dohm is not the only woman I know to reach a hundred years or better. After I became senator, two women in my own family reached that milestone, Eva McManus Crandall and Elizabeth Dunn, better known as Aunt Lizzie, and I had the pleasure of providing them both with tributes.

One time my dad told me how they got rid of the last whorehouse in Traverse City. As the story goes, at one time Traverse City had three houses of ill repute, also sometimes called bawdy houses. My dad only told me about the demise of the final one that was left. I'm not sure what part of town it stood in, but I have the idea it was on the east side of town, possibly in the Booneville, now the Traverse Heights, area. The story goes that many of the peninsula farmers used to go to town on Saturday mornings, and since they were driving horses, it wasn't unusual for them to stay in town overnight. Some of those early settlers used to frequent the whorehouses.

Old Bill Bigbee was a bachelor, never married, and he might have been a quarter of a bubble off, but he wasn't a bad fellow and in fact was well-liked by the farmers in the Archie neighborhood. Bill's claim to fame was dynamiting stumps in orchards or forests so the land could be farmed. In those days there weren't any bulldozers, so you either dug the stumps out by hand and cut the ruts off with an axe and pulled the stump with horses or you possibly hired a more sophisticated stump puller. But many fruit growers on the peninsula used to hire Bill to come dynamite their stumps.

Bill had a habit of going into town once in a while and visiting the whorehouse. As he got older, he got a little harder to accommodate and the story goes that eventually the madame had to tell him he was no longer welcome. Probably the real story was that he didn't take a bath very often and he let his whiskers grow. But that's not the way the old-timers told it!

The night he was turned away, he went home and made up his mind to get even. As he worked various dynamiting jobs that winter and spring, he accumulated half a stick of dynamite off each job. When he had enough saved up, he tied and wrapped them together and one night he went to town and set the charge underneath the front porch of the bawdy house. As he said, "I was halfway home before she went off." The dynamite blew off the front porch and the entire front part of the house and the ladies decided it was time to leave, thus ending the whorehouse days in Traverse City.

The only other time I heard a story anything like that was several years later and it didn't have anything to do with whorehouses. I was working with a group of apple growers down in the Belding area in the early years of my extension career in the late 1950s and we were putting together a fruit sales and storage organization. I got to talking with the various growers and they told me about a chivaree they'd had in that area. Chivarees in rural areas were pretty common in those days. In fact, my wife and I were chivareed the night we got home from our honeymoon. When a couple got married, you approached their house, usually after dark, and all of a sudden you let loose with the blaring of horns and all kinds of din and clamor, supposedly to wake them up, persisting until you were invited in for eats and drinks.

Down in Belding, a couple of the boys decided to have a little extra fun at the chivaree. They wrapped some dynamite much like old Bill did in wet toilet paper and got a good charge put together and set it off out in the apple orchard, kind of away from the house. It went off when the guests were inside, and was so strong it blew every window out of the house. It sent the two Whittenbach boys right off the living room couch and onto the floor.

Back when Clara and I were married in 1949, most everybody in the rural areas was chivareed. It was in late August before we went back to college and we had just gone to bed. I remember the bedroom window was open and one of my old buddies, Cal Jamieson, came right in through the window and landed in the middle of the bed! The rest of them were pounding on the door so we had to get up and let everybody in. We even had to go to the store and get some things. We weren't old enough to buy beer, but somebody got some and we had a party for most of the night, with all the neighbors sitting around talking and playing cards until they figured they had everybody completely worn out and then they got up and went home and allowed us to go back to bed. That was the usual round of doing things. It's not practiced too much anymore today, with all the problems of our modern society.

Every community has characters who have inhabited the area over the years, some good, some not so good, and some in between. Many are public-spirited citizens who work on various kinds of community activities and are very important in determining how an area is developed.

One of those on the peninsula was Mrs. W. F. Wilson, or Mrs. W. F. as we called her. Her husband's name was Willard and she was the mother of Willard Jr. and James Wilson. James Wilson was married to Agnes Courtade, who was a first cousin to my mother-in-law, so I guess in an offhand sort of way my kids are related to that end of the Wilson family, but that's not the reason for this particular story.

Mrs. W. F., who was up in years when I knew her, was an outstanding spokeswoman for the beautification of the peninsula. Her main claim to fame was that, as long as she lived, no billboards or advertising signs were allowed in Peninsula Township. None of the zoning laws or any of the various committees on top of committees they have nowadays to confuse the decision-making process existed; Mrs. W. F. simply decided there weren't going to be any billboards in Peninsula Township, so if anybody put one up, she showed up at their place and had a little conversation with them. Nobody wanted to get on the wrong side of Mrs. W. F., and in every case the sign came down.

Then Buff Kroupa, back from World War II, started a business on the corner of Carroll Road and M-37. He called it Kroupa's Station to start with; it was a Quonset building with scales for weighing fruit. Eventually it grew into a major marketing outlet for the sweet and sour cherries on the peninsula, particularly the sweet cherries, which eventually ended up in the maraschino trade. Buff did a tremendous job of providing a market for Napoleons and Golds and Windsors and other varieties of sweets that were suitable for that market. He also had a great ability to deal with the buyers of those particular commodities and to compete favorably with cherries out of Washington and Oregon and California that also ended up in that market. He also sold pesticides and fertilizers and supplies to farmers and built a big business on that corner. In short, he was a very important person in terms of the development of Peninsula Township at that time.and probably the largest sweet cherry briner in the U.S.

When he was getting up in his heyday, he decided to put a sign out in front of his place. The business was called Kroupa's, Inc. by that time and certainly nobody would question him. He was a big marketer of the growers' fruit, a good friend, and of course a peninsula native.

His dad, Bert Kroupa, was a good friend of my dad's and lived just north of Island View Road a little bit.

Nonetheless, it wasn't too long before Buff got a visit from Mrs. W. F. He thought about what she said for a few days and finally compromised with her. He had a cement block office building that sat back from the road thirty or forty feet, and he took the sign off the posts by the road and put it on the side of the building. This satisfied Mrs. W. F. and still allowed him to advertise his business.

There's a flower garden at the base of the peninsula, down where M-37 and the West Shore Road come together, dedicated to Mrs. W. F. because she did so much to keep the peninsula the beautiful place that it is, but part of the history of Mrs. W. F. I am particularly fond of goes a little bit deeper than that. When I was quite a young lad, I was at my grandmother McManuses one day when this big roadster drove into the yard with a very dignified lady in it. I don't know if you'd have called her elderly, but she was getting up in years. She was quite elegantly dressed and wore a typical matron's hat. She sort of looked like a dowager Russian empress coming into the yard.

I ran into the house and asked Grandma McManus who this person was and why she was there. Grandma told me I had to go outside and play, because that was Mrs. W. F. and she was coming for tea.

Well, it seems that Mrs. W. F. made an annual visit to my grandmother's. You'd have to know the two women to understand the contrast. Mrs. W. F. was quite well-to-do, had a successful fruit farm, had only borne a couple of kids, drove a big car, dressed elegantly, and so on, while my grandmother bore eleven kids and lived off a bunch of sand hills that never produced much money.

As I eventually learned, Mrs. W. F. was visiting my grandmother in order to collaborate on what needed to be done on the peninsula in the coming year. Mrs. W. F. was smart enough to know that if she was going to get anything done, she'd better have Eliza Jane McManus standing behind her. One thing she didn't want was Eliza Jane and her tribe standing on the other side of the fence. Grandma Mack, even though she didn't have much money or fancy clothes or the finer things in life, came from one of the oldest families on the peninsula and was the youngest daughter of Edward Carroll, whom Carroll

Road was named after. He'd been a major politician on the peninsula in his day and a highly respected fruit grower.

As I recall, the two women spent a couple of hours together that afternoon. We peeked in the windows at the two of them sitting in the living room drinking tea. Usually Grandpa and Grandma Mack drank green tea with milk, or milk and sugar, a horrible combination as far as I was concerned. I don't recall what kind of tea she served that afternoon, along with a couple of cookies, but the two of them sat there and planned how the men would handle the affairs of Peninsula Township for the year to come.

My dad always told me that even though Mrs. W. F. was quite a dowager in her own right as she got older, that's not the way she started out. It seems she had been a hired girl on the Murray farm, the same farm my mother was a hired girl on later on. Mrs. W. F. was much older than my mother, so she had been there many, many years earlier and had worked in the kitchen. In those days the Murrays were quite wealthy and had hired people live in and do those kinds of things. Bill and Jim Wilson's father started paying quite a few visits over at the Murray farm, and eventually he and Mrs. W. F. got married, but she came from rather humble beginnings. My McManus grandparents kept track of things pretty carefully. They knew what kind of background Mrs. W. F. came from, regardless of what kind of clothes she was wearing today. For her part, she was smart enough to know they weren't overly impressed by her big roadster or how many corsets she wore, and she never forgot her roots.

Another one of the characters on the peninsula was a guy I'll call Shaq, a fruit grower on the north end of the peninsula. The stories about him are myriad. Suffice it to say, he was a real character. A big man over six feet tall, he probably weighed 275 pounds. He was married to a woman from Kingsley who had been a schoolteacher and he and his wife were a little bit older than my folks. They raised a nice family of children, but Shaq himself was a wheeler and dealer. He loved to buy and sell, probably better than he enjoyed farming. He bought and sold fruit from peninsula farmers and hauled it down to the Eastern Farmers Market in Detroit. He also bought and sold cattle and hay, and he loved making it on the margin. Of course, when a man is doing that much business and dealing with lots of different people, numerous stories start circulating. One of the first ones goes that back in the Depression, he was short of money like everyone else and needed to buy groceries to feed his family so he decided to sell a pig for cash. His dad lived across the road and to the north a little bit. He had done pretty well in the fruit business and needed a pig for meat for the winter, so he went over to his son's place and asked how much they had to have for the pig. Shaq told him he wanted ten dollars for it.

"That's too much money," his dad said. "The pig's only worth five dollars. I'll give you five dollars for that pig."

Shaq said, "No, I won't sell the pig for five dollars."

His dad said "All right" and went home.

For some unknown reason, the pig died that night. Shaq got up in the morning and saw the pig was dead and went over to his dad's. He said, "The wife and I have been talking about it. We need some groceries, so I'll take your offer of five dollars for the pig."

His dad handed him the five dollars and Shaq went home and he and his wife went to town. His dad came over to get the pig and of course the pig was dead. When Shaq got back, his dad said, "I went to get the pig and it was dead. You sold me a dead pig. I want my five dollars back."

Shaq said, "You offered me the price of a dead pig and you got a dead pig. Now be satisfied."

Les Jamieson used to tell the story that Shaq and his dad were in a meeting one time with a bunch of farmers and they were all sitting around talking. Like I said, Shaq was better than six feet tall and probably 275 pounds or better. Shaq got to telling how hard up they were when he was a kid, how they never had anything, how his dad had never been able to provide him all the things he wanted, and so on. Finally he got down to the point of his story. He said things were so tough around home that after they separated the milk, they always had to sell the cream and all the family got to drink was the skim milk. When he stopped to draw a breath, his dad said, "My, Shaq, what a big boy you would have been if you'd a gotten any cream!"

Shaq got into trouble one time. The government came along and passed a bunch of laws dealing with migrant workers. Of course the farmers detested those rules and regulations. They were all providing housing for their migrants free of charge, and Traverse City was the finest place they worked the entire year. They were from south Texas, where July and August meant mostly heat, disease, and pestilence. They had a much better environment in the fruit orchards of Northern Michigan than they had at home, and they also made good money in Michigan. The farmers all knew they took their money many times to the post office in Traverse City and mailed it back to Texas to pay bills back home. Even so, the do-gooders in society, some of the church groups and other people who didn't have anything else to do, decided they were going to upgrade the migrants' conditions.

The end result was, they put the migrants out of work because the industry went to mechanical harvesting instead of utilizing the services of 35,000 migrant workers a year. Today fewer than 2,000 migrants work in the local ag industry and do nothing at all in the cherry business. I could say a lot more about all the laws. As far as the farmer is concerned, they're strictly harassment because most of the farms are small and all those regulations with their concurrent paperwork have to be implemented by the farmer or his wife. All the bookkeeping on minimum wage and workmen's compensation is typically her responsibility too. In the end, the new laws not only put the migrants out of work, many of the farmers quit as well. One thing about farming is, you don't have to do it. If you can't make a living at it, you don't. Thank God in this country farmers aren't serfs.

Shaq had some problems with the housing and regulations he wasn't following. Some of the inspectors were on to him. Then he started getting a lot of publicity, which put the rest of the farmers in kind of a tough spot. They didn't agree with the government, but they didn't like the publicity so they didn't agree with Shaq, either. The situation was at an impasse.

Shaq got called into court and old Judge Brown from Greilickville had the case. He also grew cherries and he wanted to get the case settled, but Shaq wasn't moving very fast. They had to lock him up for a day or two and they still weren't getting any action. The judge told me several years later, "You know, George, I got to thinkin' about that. His wife owned half that farm out there and I wasn't getting too far with Shaq, even puttin' him in jail, but I finally told him that as long as she owned half the farm, she'd have to go to jail with him." That was that, and they got the problem solved in short order.

Judge Brown was quite a judge. He lived to be about ninety-five. One year when I was in the extension service, I got called in as an expert witness on a case he had. The Morgan Orchards on the peninsula were owned by the John C. Morgan and Company descendants. They had the processing plant as well as the farm and they had a hired man who had died of Good Pasture disease, a disease of the kidney. His wife, influenced by her mother, decided to sue the Morgans for pesticide poisoning, hoping to collect a sizeable sum of money. Phil Clancy was the lawyer for the plaintiff and Charlie Menmuir was the lawyer for the defendants. I was called as one of the expert witnesses.

Clancy didn't know anything about spraying, so he started asking me some questions and I immediately asked him some back in terms of defining what his question was: whether it was 2x or 4x or dilute or what concentration . He didn't really have any comprehension of what the hell I was talking about. His evidence was mainly newspaper articles, which is probably the last place in the world anyone would want to look for accurate anything scientific, so he wasn't getting very far.

At that time the old Grand Traverse County Courthouse had a railing in front of the judge with a swinging door. When you walked through, it made a noise like "flip flop, flip flop." Clancy would be questioning me, and about the time he'd be getting up to make his high point, old Charlie Menmuir would walk through the gate with a piece of paper, looking very official and the gate would go "flip flop, flip flop" and the jury's attention would be drawn to that gate and they wouldn't pay a bit of attention to what Clancy said.

Things weren't going all that well for him, so he finally decided to let me down off the stand. Just as I was ready to step off, old Judge Brown said, "By the way, George, tell the jury about DDT in cherries."

I couldn't imagine what he was getting at, but I said, "We don't use any DDT in the cherries, not because we had any premonitions of *Silent Spring* or anything like that, but that particular pesticide won't kill the insects we're concerned about, cherry fruit fly and curculio, so we use other pesticides. We've never used DDT in the cherry orchards." I gave him a pretty complete explanation. When I was done, he said,

"Okay, George, I just wanted the jury to know that we don't use DDT in the cherries!"

My dad and Shaq used to haul fruit to the Detroit Farmers Market. In fact, I spent a lot of my early days there learning about marketing agricultural produce from the ground up, literally. The first time I ever drove a truck, we were hauling about two hundred bushels of apples and Shaq was driving a truck that hauled about three hundred bushels; we were both going down to the Detroit market, one following the other. I was about sixteen and riding with Dad and I didn't have a drivers' license yet. When we got down the other side of Cadillac on Highway 115, Shaq stopped us and said he was sleepy. He wanted to know if I could come back and drive his truck. My dad said he didn't want me to do that, but if Shaq was sleepy I could drive our truck and Dad would go back and drive Shaq's, while Shaq rode with me and showed me the way and supposedly kept me awake.

I'd never driven a truck on a major highway like that and I didn't have a driver's license, but that was all right; I'd driven equipment around on the farm. I got her in gear and headed down through Clare. Just about to Midland, in the dark of the night, I saw two flying red horse signs, one on each side of the road. The Mobil Oil Company in Traverse City used a flying red horse to advertise their products, but I'd never seen a sign flashing red like that. I got to thinking, why in the world would they have two Mobil Oil stations on opposite sides of the road? About that time, I noticed some interruption in the car lights coming at me and then I deciphered it was the wheels under a railroad train. Needless to say, I slammed on the brakes and got the truck stopped just before we got to the tracks. Shaq woke up and wanted to know what was the matter. I said I guessed it wasn't two flying red horse Mobil Oil stations on each side of the road; it was railroad track flashers and I'd had to stop for a train! We didn't have any train tracks on the peninsula, so I'd never seen a railroad flasher before!

He kind of grunted and we let the train go by and then I pulled on across the tracks and down the road far enough to get off on the side. I stopped and told Dad maybe he'd better drive her the rest of the way, so we let Shaq go back and take his truck on into the market.

I have to admit, Shaq knew how to deal. In 1948, he was looking for a cattle pasture and so was my dad. They both had beef cattle so they could get the manure from the cattle to use in the orchards, but they needed a place to pasture them in the summer. Shaq found out about the Ingraham ranch over in Kalkaska County, near Sharon, 1,040 acres plus another forty closer to Highway 66. He and Dad went to Chicago and bought that 1,080 acres for $8,500. It was fenced with an old house on it for a hired man and we pastured cattle there. We each put 125 head over there in the spring of the year and kept them there until fall, then sold them off and bought another bunch, wintered them on the peninsula, and then took them to Kalkaska in the spring. Invariably they would get out, or some of them would, so we spent a considerable amount of time chasing cattle in the woods over near Sharon. But eventually my dad sold his half of the land to Shaq's father, who set it up in a joint deed so Shaq eventually ended up with the whole thing. He eventually sold it to Consumers Power Company, which in turn sold it to Packaging Corporation of America.

Years later, my brothers Frank and Art and Mike put together a hunting club with about twenty-five members and repurchased that 1,040 acres. They paid something in the neighborhood of $200,000, maybe more than that, but Dad bought his half for $4,250 and sold it to Shaq's father in about 1961 or '62 for the same $4,250 and never took a profit out of that end of it. The only profit he made was on half the value with the forty acres over by Highway 66 that they sold to Elgie VanderHout for about $2,700. We did get about 350 tons of manure annually for the orchards out of the wintering of the cattle, so I guess it was all worth it. Senator Michelle McManus, Mike's daughter, is a member and hunts there as well.

Working with animals on the farm always presents challenges. It takes a great deal of patience to get them to do the things they need to do to keep life productive. Probably the best illustration of that is the story about the Quaker preacher who lived on a farm. One Sunday morning, as he was dressed up for church in his long frocked coat, the kids came up from the barn and said they were having trouble feeding the calves. Now when you've had a newborn calf, it's allowed to suck milk from the cow for the first few days to get the colostrum it needs. After that, the cow's milk is needed for human consumption and the calf has to drink from a pail. To get it to do that, it's necessary to stand over the calf and put your hand in front of its nose and put two or three fingers in its mouth. Then, coaxing its nose into the pail, the calf will taste the milk and start sucking on your fingers. Calves learn to drink quickly that way, but they have a habit of butting their heads against the pail and spilling the milk.

This Quaker preacher went down to the barn to help the kids. Sure enough, the calf butted the pail and spilled milk all over the preacher's Sunday best. In an exasperated tone, the preacher said, "If it weren't for the love of Jesus Christ, I'd break your goddamn neck." This story expresses the patience required and the exasperation experienced by most farmers who've had to deal with animals on the farm.

That reminds me of another story. A good friend of mine, one of the greatest leaders the fruit or ag industry ever had in our part of the state, liked to challenge fate now and then. He got into a program they had several years ago for bringing burros out of the Grand Canyon, where they multiplied over the years until their numbers were greater than their food supply. In other words, the government was giving away free burrows to anybody who wanted one. My friend Pete got a couple of them just for pets and kept them in his barnyard. He was always challenged by them because they had lived in the wild and were very able to protect themselves. As he said, "They could kick the gnats off the flies at fifty feet."

One day he needed to move one of the burros to a different pasture. He decided to drive his jeep and lead the burro with a rope around its neck. He secured the rope to the roll-bar just over his head by encircling the bar with the rope a couple of times and holding onto the end of it, where there was a pretty good-sized knot.

When he got down the road a little ways, the burro decided he wasn't going any further and planted all four feet. Pete wasn't expecting that and wasn't holding onto the rope tightly enough. It slipped out of his hands and unwound from the roll bar. In the process, the knot whopped him on the chin. I don't know if you've ever been whopped on the chin by a knot at the end of a rope, but it can be quite painful.

You don't get mad in such situations, you just get even. Pete backed the jeep up and put the rope around the roll bar again. This time he kept a pretty good hold on it and progressed nicely down the road. As he said, "You'd be surprised how agile one of those burros is at fifteen miles an hour movin' down the highway!"

My dad told me a couple of stories about working with horses, which I never really did a whole lot of. We had a team at home and I drove them a few times, but we weren't allowed around them much when we were young because my mother didn't trust them. By the time we were old enough to handle them, we were moving into tractors.

My dad, of course, drove horses all his life. He used a lot of psychology to try to stay one step ahead of them and get the job done. He told me about a team he once had in which one of the horses tended to be balky. It would pull all right on level ground, but anytime you came to a hill that looked like it would take extra effort, old Duke would balk. Well, the old man came up with a way to handle that. He was pulling a load of gravel and he continued up the road until he got just a few seconds from where Duke usually balked. There he stopped the team and said "Gee," which means go to the right. He drove as far to the right as they could go with the wagon sitting still. He followed that by saying "Haw," which means go left as far as you can.

He continued to say "Gee" and "Haw" without letting 'em go anywhere until pretty soon he could see the sweat standing out on old Duke's neck. When he figured he'd had about enough of that, he pulled the horses back to where the tongue was centered with the road and said "Git up" and they went right up over the hill and Duke didn't have any problem with it at all. I suppose that's where the saying comes that you need to make them sweat a little sometimes to get things done.

Another story Dad told me confused me for a while, but later I began to see the wisdom of it. He had a different team with a horse that used to jump when he got ready to pull a load. Instead of making a nice even pull like a pullin' horse should, he tended to rare and jump ahead, in which case his partner on the other side would fall back and things would end up in a general state of confusion. Dad got to analyzing what it would take to straighten the situation out and decided a little sharp poke in the rear at the right time would do it, so he went over to the woods and cut a little pole about two feet long. He took his jack knife and sharpened the end of it to a good point and got behind the horse that wasn't the problem and said, "Get up."

When the horse on the right jumped, he jabbed the other horse in the rear and it jumped too. I suppose that illustrates the point that, once in a while, you've got to jab the innocent in the right spot in order to keep the guilty in line!

Many more stories could be told about farming and about various characters on the Old Mission Peninsula and even confined to the Archie neighborhood, but these are just a few I recall at the moment. The same is true for those in my extension and political careers. Time and space do not permit them all here, but I need to apologize to all those who have been left out. It was not by any particular design or plan, simply my own recall at the time of this writing.

About the Author

George McManus Jr. was born into a farming family on the Old Mission Peninsula just outside of Traverse City, Michigan. With agriculture in his blood, he graduated from Michigan State College with bachelor's and master's degrees in horticulture with a minor in agricultural economics. He put these degrees to good use in his twenty-five-plus years with Michigan State University's Cooperative Extension Service. In these same years, with the help of his father, he acquired the fruit farm he and his wife Clara still own today just south of Traverse City. There they raised nine children and began developing their cherry orchards.

During his final years with extension, George began his numerous public service activities in Traverse City and the state of Michigan. Just a few highlights: he served four terms as a trustee to the Northwestern Michigan College board; he was appointed to the Michigan Agricultural Commission by Governor James Blanchard, where he served six years; he was an active Rotarian, serving one year as president of the Traverse City club and participating in the annual Rotary Show and ultimately as secretary of the board of Rotary Charities; he sat on the board of the Traverse City Chamber of Commerce, serving one year as board chairman; and he served on the school board of the Grand Traverse Area Catholic Schools. In 1990, his commitment to public service culminated in his election to the Michigan Senate, where he served until 2002, when he was term-limited out.

Whether farming cherries, educating other farmers through his extension work, raising kids, or serving the public at large, George McManus has remained close to his roots and committed to serving others while taking care of the land.